Collapse and Rebirth of Cultural Heritage

GLOBAL POLITICS AND SECURITY

Volume 6

Edited by

Prof. Lorenzo Kamel,
University of Turin's History Department,
and Istituto Affari Internazionali (IAI)

PETER LANG

Bern · Berlin · Bruxelles · New York · Oxford

Lorenzo Kamel (ed.)

Collapse and Rebirth of Cultural Heritage

The Case of Syria and Iraq

PETER LANG

Bern · Berlin · Bruxelles · New York · Oxford

Bibliographic Information published by the Deutsche Nationalbibliothek
The Deutsche Nationalbibliothek lists this publication in the Deutsche Nationalbibliografie; detailed bibliographic data is available in the internet at http://dnb.d-nb.de.

Library of Congress Cataloging-in-Publication Data
A CIP catalog record for this book has been applied for at the Library of Congress.

The publication of this book has relied upon the cooperation and support of the Compagnia di San Paolo, the Istituto Affari Internazionali (IAI), the Italian Ministry of Foreign Affairs and International Cooperation, the German Marshall Fund (GMF) of the United States, the Organization for Security and Co-operation in Europe (OSCE), and the University of Turin's History Department. The opinions expressed in this volume are those of the editor and the authors, and do not necessarily reflect the official policy or position of any of the above mentioned institutions or think tanks.

Cover Image: © Stefano Zaccaria/Shutterstock.com

ISSN 2624-8905 • ISBN 978-3-0343-4127-1 (Print)
E-ISBN 978-3-0343-4135-6 (E-PDF) • E-ISBN 978-3-0343-4136-3 (EPUB)
E-ISBN 978-3-0343-4137-0 (MOBI) • DOI 10.3726/b17248

Wabernstrasse 40, CH-3007 Bern, Switzerland
bern@peterlang.com, www.peterlang.com

This publication has been peer reviewed.

www.peterlang.com

Contents

Figures

Tables

Ettore Greco and Nicolò Russo Perez

Foreword

In the last two decades several countries in the Middle East and North Africa have been ravaged by bloody and protracted armed conflicts that have caused appalling humanitarian crises and widespread destruction of infrastructures and basic public services. Their economies and the entire social fabric have been severely hit. Creating the conditions for recovery from these wide-ranging disruptions remains a daunting challenge, not least because, even in the areas where a degree of stability has been achieved, worrying conflict factors remain at work.

Cultural heritage, which is a vital component of human activity and a strategic resource for economic and social development, has not been spared. Armed hostilities, often conducted with heavy weapons, have destroyed a great number of historical monuments and artefacts. Moreover, many manifestations and symbols of cultural heritage have become the specific target of extremist and terrorist groups inspired by exclusivist or nihilist ideologies. What is at stake now is no less than the preservation of complex cultural identities in a region which has itself been the cradle of civilizations and religions.

This volume, edited by Lorenzo Kamel, examines the economic, social, political and cultural impact of the damage inflicted to the cultural heritage of the Middle East in the course of the recent armed conflicts which have involved both local actors – state and sub-state – and regional and external powers. The volume examines the cases of Iraq and Syria, which have been at the centre of prolonged wars and civil conflicts – Iraq since 2003, Syria since 2011 – with a focus on the devastating consequences for the archaeological patrimony of such culturally rich cities as Aleppo, Baghdad and Mosul.

Collapse and Rebirth of Cultural Heritage looks into the role that the now damaged archaeological sites played in the formation of historical and social identities, emphasizing the importance of the ongoing reconstruction plans for safeguarding the cultural identity of the local population and enabling it to resume normal social life. Several initiatives have been launched but they have often come up against obstacles stemming from endemic political instability and deep-seated ethnic and religious rivalries, which hinders cooperation and the mobilization of resources. The volume offers an in-depth analysis, in particular, of the recovery processes of highly symbolic sites such as the Ancient City of

Aleppo and the Iraq National Museum in Baghdad, focusing on the actual and potential synergies between local actors and international organizations.

Only recently has the reconstruction of damaged cultural heritage become a central component of the mandate of the international organizations and peace-keeping missions working on post-conflict reconstruction and rehabilitation. The UN Security Council Resolution 2437 approved in March 2017 provides the political and legal basis for the integration of a cultural dimension into UN peace-keeping operations. The United Nations Educational, Scientific and Cultural Organization (UNESCO) has been a driving force in promoting the preservation of cultural heritage as part and parcel of the international action to maintain peace and security in the world, but other institutional actors, in particular the World Bank, have also play a prominent role. No doubt, the cultural rebirth of the conflict-ravaged areas of the region will continue to require long-lasting international efforts and will put to test, in the coming decades, the capacity of the relevant international actors to provide tailor-made support that takes into account the cultural specificities of each area and establishes a functional relationship with the local population.

National governments also have crucial responsibilities for providing essential resources and expertise. The volume emphasizes the pioneering initiatives undertaken by Italy. In 2016 Unesco and the Italian government reached an agreement for the establishment of the unite4Heritage taskforce based on a special unit of the Italian Carabinieri specialized in the protection of cultural heritage. In the same year, Italy and Iraq created a joint cultural institute for archaeology and the restoration of monuments. Thanks also to these new instruments Italy has made a significant contribution to the international initiative to preserve the cultural heritage of Iraq. This action needs to be coupled with a more intense fight against the trade of antiquities, looted or stolen, from archeological sites. This edited volume devotes special attention to the responsibilities of academics working with collectors and dealers, presenting several case studies that show how academic studies can sometimes facilitate the acquisition of antiquities illicitly acquired.

The protection of cultural heritage has also come to be seen as an integral part of the global strategy against terrorism. Indeed, several terrorist groups pursued the objective of annihilating what they stigmatized as illegitimate or apostate cultures by destroying artefacts and monuments giving testimony to their historical roots and value. However, as emphasized in this work, it is essential that the interventions to preserve cultural heritage at risk or under direct attack are not tarnished, in the eyes of the local population, by cultural bias emphasizing a presumed superiority of Western cultural values or traditions. This can play into the hands of anti-West extremist groups. Three chapters, in particular, highlight the negative impact that distorted concepts or images of Middle Eastern cultures may have on the effectiveness of international action to safeguard cultural heritage.

By offering such comprehensive analysis of the problems and potentialities of the protection of cultural heritage in the Middle East, this edited book makes a valuable contribution to the deeper understanding of an area of international cooperation that is of growing importance for both the advancement of individual and social rights and the maintenance of international peace.

Lorenzo Kamel

Introduction

On 17 October 2019, the Rectorate Hall of the University Turin hosted a New-Med conference entitled 'Cultural Heritage and Illicit Trafficking in a Fragmented Middle East'. The meeting, organized jointly by the University of Turin's Department of Historical Studies and the Istituto Affari Internazionali (IAI), relied upon the cooperation and support of the Compagnia di San Paolo, the Italian Ministry of Foreign Affairs and International Cooperation, the German Marshall Fund (GMF) of the United States and the Organization for Security and Co-operation in Europe (OSCE).

Some twenty-four international renowned scholars, head of museums, practitioners, and policy makers from eleven countries gathered to analyze the dramatic events that have affected cultural heritage in Middle Eastern countries in recent years. Speakers also focused on the human dimension of this tragedy and shed light on projects seeking to renew cultural heritage in the region, including museums, archaeological excavations and the restoration of damaged monuments.

This edited volume builds on some of the results of that successful conference and aims primarily to raise awareness of cultural heritage, with particular focus on the Iraqi and Syrian contexts.

To this end, Chapter 1, by Elijah J. Magnier, Al-Rai chief correspondent and veteran war correspondent, provides the regional background and sheds light on the main roots of the process of destabilization that has affected several countries of the Middle East in recent years. The author, who has worked in war zones in the region for over three decades, contends that the rebirth of cultural heritage in Iraq and Syria will only be possible when violent and extremist jihadists are defeated, stability is restored, and an acceptable degree of recovery of the economy has been achieved. These are still distant objectives due to the well-established, corrupt political system, the weakness of the central government in Baghdad and the lack of national reconciliation in both Iraq and Syria. Moreover, according to Magnier, US–Iran animosity continues to transform Iraq and Syria into a battlefield, effectively contributing to the instability of both Middle Eastern countries.

The second chapter, written by the former Director of the UNESCO World Heritage Centre, Francesco Bandarin, examines the current strategies for the reconstruction and recovery of Aleppo, within the broader framework of the reorganization of civilian life in Syria after the conflict. The author points out that most of this ancient city was completely destroyed during four years of fighting: all its major monuments have suffered major damage. While the current political situation does not allow for recovery to be achieved quickly, the process of reconstruction and recovery of the Old City of Aleppo has begun, and attempts have been made to establish a medium- and long-term strategy for the reconstruction and recovery of the city, as expressed in the document 'Vision and Planning Framework', recently submitted to the UNESCO World Heritage Committee. Bandarin assesses the implications and potential of such endeavours.

In Chapter 3, Stefano de Martino, a professor of Hittitology at the University of Turin, turns attention to the Archaeological Museum in Baghdad as a symbol of Iraqi cultural identity. The political use of Mesopotamian heritage made by Saddam Hussein manipulated the perception of the Iraqi past, with the purpose of supporting his aggressive strategies against neighbouring countries. In the days and years following Saddam's fall (April 2003), the Museum was sacked and many artefacts were either stolen or damaged. Against this backdrop, the author discusses the crucial yet relatively little-known role played by the Carabinieri Corps, the Centro Scavi e Ricerche di Torino per il Medio Oriente e l'Asia and the University of Bologna in supporting Iraqi archaeologists and the multi-ethnic and multi-cultural traditions of their country.

The fourth chapter, by Omar Mohammed, a historian from Mosul who was known until 2017 as the anonymous blogger 'Mosul Eye', provides a timely analysis on the ties between cultural heritage and cultural identity. The author provides examples of Mosul's cultural heritage and demolished historical sites, while shedding light on the discussions that they have triggered in the city since ISIS occupation in August 2014. Mohammed reminds us that the city of Mosul has experienced almost 300 invasions by various foreign nations and empires. Nevertheless, it has always protected its cultural heritage and identity, whether through language, literature or visual memory.

In Chapter 5, Abdul Salam Taha, an Iraqi archaeologist who has worked for several years to support the protection of cultural heritage in his country, focuses on the involvement of academicians in illicitly traded cultural heritage artefacts and documents which belong to war-torn states. Referring to a number of case studies, the author explores how a certain number of scholars use their knowledge and expertise to serve private collectors, museums and even, sometimes, auction houses. In doing so, he sheds light on how such scholars tend to erase the role and value of culturally sensitive items for the collective memory and identity of suffering nations.

My own final chapter points out that cultural heritage is not only a relatively new idea – deeply rooted in the nineteenth century, when Europeans showed an increasing interest in preserving medieval buildings – but also a problematic one. It is, in fact, a top-down ideal usually defined by the most powerful members of society. To counter this, a number of interested observers have stressed the need to democratize cultural heritage, giving greater control to local communities. I contend that the 'democratization' of cultural heritage should be coupled, on a more theoretical level, with a process of 'de-Westernization' that builds on a more informed awareness about the process of 'accumulation' which underpins many of the achievements, ideals, and perceptions that lie at the very base of much of what we commonly consider as tangible (such as works of art, artefacts, books) and intangible culture (such as knowledge, folklore and traditions).

Elijah J. Magnier

Chapter 1: The Steep Cost of Destabilizing Iraq and Syria

Every American president since Jimmy Carter has declared 'war on terror', a war that has been not merely a 'clash of civilizations' (MacDonald et al. 2012: 118). Rather, it has been, and remains, an ill-conceived strategy, because it has aimed to fight the former Soviet Union's expansion and hegemony and control the very rich energy sources in the Middle East, without foreseeing the devastating consequences of such a strategy for the region's populations and their cultural heritage (Chomsky 2008: 162–3).

The 1979 Soviet invasion of Afghanistan, an ambush of the type the United States suffered in Vietnam, dragged Moscow into a quagmire (Brzezinski 1983: 429; see also Gibbs 2000: 241–2). The arming of the Afghan and Arab Mujahedeen and their victory over the Soviets in Afghanistan gave them the necessary boost to attract thousands of jihadist followers with the objective of establishing an 'Islamic state' (Islamic Emirate or Caliphate) in the Middle East and Central Asia. The 'warriors of peace' (Fisk 1993) appeared to be the worst enemies of ancient and modern civilization.[1] They advocated the return of the ancient glory of Islam, according to their own interpretation of glory and of Islam.

When the Taliban Mujahedeen took power, they presented the world with an example of the kind of rule to expect. Not only did the Taliban carry out indiscriminate killings (Girardet 2011: 306), violate human rights and deprive women of access to knowledge, they also demonstrated their capacity to destroy ancient artefacts of world heritage (Strick van Linschoten and Kuehn 2018: 257). The destruction of the Buddhas of Bamiyan, for example, aimed to eradicate all cultural inheritance foreign to the Taliban ideology (Wyndham 2015: 122).

The effective US plan to draw the Soviets into a devastating war in Afghanistan was followed by the Soviet policy of Perestroika. The process of decline and

1 See US Secretary of State Hillary Clinton's testimony before Congress on 23 April 2009: 'Let's remember here the people we are fighting today we funded 20 years ago. [. . .] let's go recruit these Mujahideen and let's get some to come from Saudi Arabia and other places, importing their Wahhabi brand of Islam so that we can go beat the Soviet Union' (US Congress 2010).

dispersion of the former Soviet Union then began in earnest. The US objective for Afghanistan was to drain the Soviet Union's resources and force it to withdraw without achieving its objective. This was accomplished, but not without a heavy price: the birth of al-Qaeda.

Following the invasion of Iraq in 2003, the United States was caught up in a challenging war with an unexpected outcome: hundreds of thousands were killed (Rawaf 2013). The country was also confronted with another, more lethal jihadist group than was previously known: al-Qaeda in Iraq,[2] which metamorphosed into a killing machine under the name 'Islamic State of Iraq', and later the 'Islamic State of Iraq and Syria', ISIS (Bunzel 2015). Less than a decade later, ISIS occupied a third of Iraq (Hamasaeed and Nada 2019).

The partition of Iraq into three sub-states (Sunni, Shia and Kurdish) was on the table. ISIS committed mass killings among various ethnic and religious groups, but also followed the example of the Taliban by levelling 1,000 columns, over 500 tombs and a Roman aqueduct along with the 2,000-year-old Temple of Bel (or Baal) in Palmyra, Syria, from the seventh century BCE (Barnard and Saad 2015). Also destroyed were the Gateway of the ancient Assyrian city of Nineveh (also known as the 'Gate of God') in Iraq and numerous other irreplaceable artefacts (Worley 2016). The brutality manifested by ISIS during its rule is leading societies in Iraq and Syria to reject the group and no longer rally behind it, as was the case prior to 2014.

However, the rebirth of the cultural heritage in Iraq and Syria requires stability and security in both countries. The heavy sanctions imposed on Syria and the instability of the Iraqi government must first be addressed before recovering what has been stolen and sold on the international market, actively restoring

---

2 Abu Musab al-Zarqawi led Jamaat al-Tawid wal-Jihad in 1999. He declared his loyalty to al-Qaeda Central led by Osama bin Laden and renamed the group he led in Iraq as *Tanzim Qaidat al-Jihad fi bilad al-Rafidayn* (al-Qaeda in Iraq, AQI) in 2004. In 2006, the group was renamed *Majlis Shura al-Mujahedeen*. Following the death of Zarqawi, it was renamed as *Dawlat al-Iraq al-Islamiya* (Islamic State of Iraq, ISI). It kept the same name until 2013 when the Emir of the group Abu Bakr al-Baghdadi announced the expansion of ISI to Syria. ISI became *al-Dawla al-Islamiya fil-Iraq wal Sham* (Islamic State of Iraq and Sham, ISIS). *Sham* stands for the ancient name of the Levant, a region encompassing Syria and Lebanon, or the modern name of Syria, but also used to indicate the city of Damascus. In mid-2014, following the occupation of Mosul and a third of Iraq, Baghdadi declared the 'Islamic Caliphate'. The group was indicated as *al-Dawla al-Islamiya* (the Islamic State, IS) but was also called ISIS, ISIL or Daesh. Daesh is the Arabic acronym despised by the members of the group.

what the jihadists have destroyed and preserving the priceless world heritage sites and artefacts of ancient civilizations.

Alas, Iraqi politicians have been involved in mass corruption, mismanagement, nepotism and incompetence, unconcerned with the needs of the population and with little awareness of their struggles (Magnier 2019b). Moreover, Iraqi political leaders have been divided over their differing loyalties to the United States, Iran and other nearby countries, rather than striving for integrity and national unity.

The relationship between Iraq and Iran suffers most when Iran intervenes in Iraqi political decisions and pushes the country towards a negative stance against the United States. Moreover, the relationship between the Iraqi government and the US administration turned sour in a radical fashion when in July 2019 Israel bombed several warehouses in Iraq; in December 2019, the US Air Force bombed five Iraqi security forces bases based on the Iraqi–Syrian border; and in January 2020, a US drone strike killed an Iraqi high commander, Abu Mahdi al-Muhandis, and an Iranian envoy, Major General Qassem Soleimani (Bowen 2020).

In addition, Iran used the influence it has among many local Iraqi groups to fight the United States through these allies. These actions undermined the sovereignty of Iraq, pushing the Middle East to the edge of war (Magnier 2019a). The site of the struggle was not limited to Iraq alone. In fact, the US plan to create a 'new Middle East' (Beauchamp 2015) involved the conquest of Lebanon, Libya, Iran, Iraq, Syria and other countries of the region (Jaffer 2019).

Nine years of war have destroyed Syria's infrastructure and left hundreds of thousands dead or wounded. The continuing occupation of the oil-rich northeast of Syria, the encouragement to the Syrian Kurds to remain distant from the central government in Damascus, the blockade of the border crossing between Iraq and Syria at al-Tanf, the prevention of the return of diplomatic missions from other Arab countries and the tight control of Syrian exports through the Jordanian borders all contributed to crippling the local economy in a country whose military forces have been fighting on several fronts for nine years to impose and maintain sovereignty and independence.

Moreover, the war in Syria has brought to its territory tens of thousands of jihadists, two superpowers (Russia and the United States) operating on the same soil in the same airspace, two powerful regional countries (Turkey and Iran) both wanting their share, and many militia groups from Lebanon, Iraq, Pakistan, Afghanistan and elsewhere. All these elements have contributed to instability, in Syria in particular and in the Levant in general. There are no indications that any of these players will leave Syria anytime soon.

The instability in Iraq and Syria has affected, and will continue to affect, the general well-being of the Middle East and even the nearby European continent. The precariousness weighs on the local population, turning life into a struggle for survival. Further wars and further impoverishment of the inhabitants leading to out-migration have become strong possibilities in the midst of the financial instability hitting the Levant and the expenses accrued due to the recent wars. Moreover, the Israeli bombing of hundreds of targets in both Syria and Iraq comprises an additional factor contributing to the volatility of the region.

Meanwhile, dozens of archaeological sites have been either looted or destroyed. The process of recovering this world heritage wealth has not yet begun, nor is it high among the country's priorities at the moment, since Syria is still at war and its army is still involved in combat.

1.1 The destabilization of Iraq

Ansar al-Islam, the Kurdistan branch of al-Qaeda, was well established in Kurdistan before the United States occupation of Iraq in 2003 (Bakawan 2017: 13–7). When the United States invaded Iraq, the jihadist group moved from out of Kurdistan and declared loyalty to Osama bin Laden to become al-Qaeda in Iraq (AQI). By 2004 AQI led by Abu Musab al-Zarqawi (Michael 2007) became well established in the Anbar Sunni western province and the northern province of Nineveh, in particular in the second biggest city of Iraq, Mosul. By 2008 the Islamic State of Iraq (ISI, formerly AQI) was running a fully organized extortion racket, earning enough money to sustain a much larger insurgency against the Iraqi forces (Whiteside 2015).

The 'war on terror' provided an opportunity for jihadists to gather together in a safe place with the entire al-Qaeda leadership (Chulov 2014), including Abu Bakr al-Baghdadi, the leader of the Islamic State of Iraq and Syria (ISIS) (Daly 2017). Thousands of Islamists were imprisoned in a secure place, at the US detention centre Camp Bucca, including Baghdadi and one of his lieutenants, Abu Mohammad al-Joulani (2006) (Atwan 2015: 32–58; Alkaff and Bin Jani 2016), who later moved from Iraq to lead the al-Qaeda branch in Syria. Camp Bucca was a detention facility maintained by the United States military in the vicinity of Umm Qasr, Iraq, came to be known as the 'Jihadist University' (McCoy 2014; Arango and Schmitt 2014).

In 2014, ISIS and several Sunni groups (jihadist Salafist like Ansar al-Sunna and the Army of the Mujahedeen; nationalist Salafist like the Islamic Army; and former Baathist groups like the 1920 Revolt Brigades and Jaish al-Tariqa al-Naqshabandiya) (Abu Rumman 2008) occupied the northern Iraqi city of Mosul (Whiteside 2017). There was a potential plan to divide up Iraq with the consent of the US, of neighbouring countries like Turkey and Saudi Arabia (Cooper 2007), and of many Sunni and Kurdish Iraqis willing to have the country disassembled and thus have their own state in Kurdistan, the Sunni Anbar and Nineveh (Biden and Gelb 2006).

Academic and mainstream media inaccurately argue that Mosul fell because the 'Sunnis grew frustrated with Maliki's sectarian rule' (Parker et al. 2014). Neighbouring Turkey, and many Iraqis including Iraqi Kurdish leader Masoud Barzani, hailed and approved ISIS and the other Sunni groups' occupation of the second largest Iraqi city and described it as a Sunni 'revolution of the oppressed' (Shafaaq 2014). Turkey retained its influence through the governor of Mosul, Atheel al-Nujaifi (Mogelson 2016), and even after the fall of the city kept 49 diplomats at the consulate, seemingly with no fear for their lives (Hubbard et al. 2014). The Kurds, led by Masoud Barzani, took full control of the oil-rich city of Kirkuk (Goudsouzian and Fatah 2014) and believed ISIS and the other Sunni groups would pave the way for the partition of Iraq and contribute to the birth of Kurdistan (Chamytelli and Coles 2016).

When ISIS overwhelmed all the other Sunni groups and took full control of the insurgency, it managed to occupy a third of Iraq. This unlawful occupation of Iraq (Kramer et al. 2015; on the non-existence of weapons of mass destruction, see Mortimer 2017) turned the country into a massive battlefield.

The US troops and political leadership were not prepared to restore stability in Iraq. Being able to manage a Middle Eastern civilization after occupying it with a western army is far from guaranteed in the twenty-first century. Indeed, to illustrate the gap, when it invaded Afghanistan in 2001, the US Army was surprised to discover how many military personnel there spoke Pashtu (Ledeen 2002: 53–94).

Although robust intelligence anticipated the potentiality of ISIS spreading in Iraq and expanding into Syria, little was done to prevent it (Flynn 2016). Iraqi sovereignty was endangered and the unity of the country and the well-being of Iraqi society became 'fragilized'. The growing power of the anti-government Sunni groups, including the former al-Qaeda ISIS, seems to have been noticed but was allowed to manifest itself for reasons that remain unclear. Many academics and researchers also continue to ignore this critical factor (Strachan 2017).

In the midst of this chaotic situation, the Sunni groups, nationalists and violent extremists joined forces and gained ground in the northern provinces, reaching the gates of Baghdad. At that point the highest Shia religious authority, the Grand Ayatollah Sayyed Ali al-Sistani, based in Najaf (Oweis 2020), agreed to the formation of a Popular Mobilization Force (PMF, '*al-Hashd al-Shaabi*' in Arabic). He made this decision after receiving a visit from an Iranian envoy, the head of the Iranian Revolutionary Guard Corps (IRGC)–Quds Brigade (Uskowi 2019), Major General Qassem Soleimani. Although the majority of the PMF are Shia, other Sunni and Christians joined in to liberate their homes from ISIS.

Iran was concerned about a possible ISIS victory due to its long border with Iraq and the imminent danger a powerful terrorist group represented for Iranian national security. Moreover, it later became clear that the consequences of the expansion of ISIS and other Sunni groups represented a previously unforeseen golden opportunity for Iran to put faithful groups holding the same ideology as the Iraqis on its payroll. The PMF needed weapons, and the opportunity was too tempting for Iran not to step in; thus, it has supplied Iraqis who are willing to fight ISIS with weapons and advisors (Schmitt 2015).

Iraq boasts many of Shia Islam's most sacred shrines (Fuller and Francke 2001), including the Karbala shrine constructed in AD 680 (Black 2017). Both Iran and Iraq feared the destruction of their holy shrines should ISIS prevail. Already in 2005, the former al-Qaeda in Iraq had destroyed (Delanghe 2008: 197) the holy sepulchres of Imams Ali Al-Hadi and Hassan Al-Askari shrine, which triggered unprecedented sectarian violence. The shrine is registered in both the World Heritage list and the World Heritage in Danger list. ISIS did not hesitate to destroy the Mosul Library and to burn thousands of rare books of philosophy, law, science and poetry. UNESCO (2015) called it a 'cultural cleansing' and 'one of the most devastating acts of destruction of library collections in human history'. ISIS also vandalized museums and artefacts and bulldozed the Mosque of the Prophets of Yunus and Jerjis in Nineveh. It also caused serious damage to the best-preserved UNESCO World Heritage Parthian city of Hatra, in the Nineveh governorate, by destroying sculptures, walls and engravings using explosives and bulldozers (Heing 2018: 54–6).

The delay in delivering already-paid-for weapons to the Iraqis gave ISIS an advantage. Western companies benefited from Iraqi wealth but contributed little to the country's progress and the rebuilding of its infrastructure. Additionally, the extreme degree of corruption among Iraqi politicians increased the level of bitterness among the population. US military training proved of little value when Sunni rebels and ISIS occupied Mosul. The disordered and chaotic withdrawal of Iraqi forces from Mosul resulted in thousands of troops being killed (Verini 2019). Moreover, the government in Baghdad failed to appoint competent commanders to lead the security forces and keep them united. Cousins and tribal followers of (former) Prime Minister Nuri al-Maliki were even appointed to the most sensitive and highest command positions within the Mosul army and intelligence service.

Iraqi political leaders, mainly Shia, were bickering among themselves over power and dominance in Baghdad. They had given their vote to a prime minister who undermined even his own cabinet members and who had the final say in all state affairs. Iran supported al-Maliki for a second term because he promised to secure the total US withdrawal from Iraq.

The stability of Iraq is important, but it is particularly crucial to Iran for a number of reasons. The Shia are a majority in Iraq and represent a huge community in harmony with the Iranian Shia. Pilgrimage tourism between Iran and Iraq allows tens of millions to travel between the two countries, where both sets of inhabitants visit their respective holy shrines. US sanctions on Iran mean that Iranian sales of merchandise, oil and gas through Iraq are a significant source of income in foreign currency, particularly since Iran has been subject to the US 'maximum pressure' sanctions (Rosemberg 2019).

Creating the PMF was the only way to stop ISIS and allow time for the security forces to recover their strength. Iran played an important role in defeating ISIS and in arming the PMF to fight and win the difficult battle along with all the other security forces and partners of Iraq in the war. Iran rushed to support not only the Shia but also the Kurds so they could defend their cities (Coles 2014). Tehran was gathering allies not only among the Shia but also the Kurds to consolidate its influence in Iraq.

Nevertheless, Iran made and still makes the mistake of supporting non-state actors when it could have enjoyed an excellent relationship with the central government in Baghdad. This is one of the biggest issues Iran fails to understand; the Iranians thought that by creating a mirror image of the IRGC in Iraq, they could transform the country into an ideological state similar to the 'Islamic Republic of Iran'. Both the United States and Iran, from opposite sides, have failed to understand the limits of what is possible in Iraq and how to manage the Iraqis (Magnier 2018).

Following the defeat of ISIS, the United States redeployed its forces in Iraq at the request of the Iraqi government. However, the PMF was demonized because it represented a danger to the US monopoly in Iraq. The Shia majority volunteers within the PMF were trained not only in the use of weapons, they were also indoctrinated with a strong ideology to stand, fight and hold their ground against the Sunni violent extremist ideology of ISIS.

Sunni Islamic groups who declared Jihad and promoted armed struggle believed in killing the Shia[3] as part of their creed and the Islamic teaching they have adopted from their favourite 13th century theologian Sheikh al-Islam Taqi al-Din Ahmad, better known as Ibn Taymiyya (Bori 2004).

The PMF is highly motivated to protect the country against ISIS and any other foreign force, including the United States, which represents a danger to Iraq's sovereignty. Moreover, Iran's efforts gained momentum in supporting any group that was faithful to its anti-US cause. ISIS was eventually expelled from every single Iraqi city, and the Iraqi government officially integrated the PMF into its security forces under the direct command of the prime minister.

The US administration recognised but failed to correctly interpret the level of discontent among a part of the Iraqi Shia towards Iran. The United States seemed to believe that allowing Israeli jets to violate Iraqi airspace (Times of Israel 2020), repeatedly bombing the PMF brigade positions and destroying weapons warehouses, would not trigger a general reaction, or perhaps would go unnoticed by the core population and even probably by the highest religious authority, the Marjaiya, in the city of Najaf (Rubin and Bergman 2019). Moreover, with the United States dominating the sky over Iraq, Israeli drones were able to kill an Iraqi commander who was leading the war on ISIS stragglers on the borders with Syria.

These acts of war were far from beneficial to the United States in Iraq. Understanding the Iraqi dynamic is vital for any country with a substantial interest in Iraq. The US approach indicated that its interpretation of the possible reactions and mood of the population in Iraq was erroneous.

---

3 See Zarqawi letter to al-Qaeda Central intercepted by the Coalition Provisional Authority: '3 [sic]. The Shi`a [. . .] "They are the enemy. Beware of them." Shaykh al-Islam Ibn Taymiyya spoke with truth and honesty when he said - after he mentioned their (Shi`a) thinking toward the people of Islam – "For this reason, with their malice and cunning, they help the infidels against the Muslim mass[es] [. . .]. Their greatest [act of] worship is to curse the Muslim friends of God from first to last. [. . .] If the Muslims defeat the Christians and polytheists, this causes distress among the Shi'a. And if the polytheists and Christians beat the Muslims, this occasions [sic] a holiday and joy among the Shi`a.' – al-Fatawa, part 28, pages 478 to 527 [. . .] Praise be to God, it is as if veils had been lifted from the hidden for him (Ibn Taymiyya) [...]. Our imams have traced a clear path and lifted the veil from these people. Imam al-Bukhari says, not in the house have I prayed behind a Shi`i or behind Jews or Christians. They are not to be greeted. They are not to be congratulated on holidays. They are not to be taken in marriage. They cannot bear witness. The animals they slaughter are not to be eaten. – Khalq Af`al al-'Ibad, page 125' (Zarkawi 2004).

Indeed, in a surprising attack, US forces struck five Iraqi security forces targets based on the Iraqi–Syrian border, killing or wounding seventy-nine officers and soldiers (Barnes 2019). It is a serious matter when even an ally of Iraq (the United States) starts to kill Iraqi forces. This violation of the terms and regulations of the US presence in Iraq was a strong indication of the weakness of the central government in Baghdad. The United States justified its attack as a response to the killing of a US-national translator. The United States accused the Iraqi Shia forces of bombing a US base, the K1 (Rubin 2020). But the bombing took place from an area situated in the heart of a Sunni-controlled area famous for attacks by ISIS, making it – according to Iraqi intelligence officers – highly unlikely that Shia forces were operating from there. The United States failed to offer evidence for its claim. The retaliation took place against Iraqi officers based 550 kilometres away from the Kirkuk-K1 base where the US contractor was killed (Magnier 2019c).

Events were rapidly unfolding in Iraq. The US decision to assassinate Iranian Major General Qassem Soleimani and Iraqi commander Abu Mahdi al-Muhandis with their companions at Baghdad airport (Magnier 2020) may be considered unlawful if no proof of imminent danger to US interests or personnel is presented (Lister and Brower 2020). To date, the United States has produced no evidence of any imminent attack justifying the targeted killing (Baker and Gibbons-Neff 2020). The US president does not seem to be interested because it 'doesn't really matter' (Gittleson 2020). The assassination killed not only an Iraqi commander but also a high-ranking Iranian officer, Major General Soleimani, who was also an envoy of his government to Iraq and a diplomat with full immunity. Soleimani was acting as an official advisor to the Iraqi government in its war with ISIS (Roggio and Toumaj 2016).

Iran made advantageous use of the consequences of the targeted killing of its general. And the US attack seems to have united the previously divided Iraqi politicians, who gathered under one leader, Sayyed Moqtada al-Sadr, at the request of Iran (Coles 2020). Iranian leaders took the opportunity to rally their own population to reinforce national unity and increase the level of animosity towards the United States. Iran retaliated against the largest US military base in Iraq, Ayn al-Assad, causing serious damage to the infrastructure and over a hundred casualties among US service personnel (Correll 2020).

US President Donald Trump threatened to bomb Iran's cultural heritage sites, expressing little concern about the possible consequences of such an act for World Heritage sites (Jakes 2020).[4] President Trump threatened to destroy

4 In the sixth century (550–330 BCE), Iran was host to the Achaemenids-Pars, the world's first ancient empire, founded by Cyrus the Great, which ruled parts of the

not only twenty-two, but fifty-two Iranian cultural heritage sites in a *bras de fer* between Washington and Tehran, with the battlefield spreading to Iraq, Syria and beyond (Yeung 2020). Iran would retaliate against US military bases in Iraq but also in nearby countries (Holmes 2020). Iraq had become a battlefield between the United States and Iran.

During the 2003 occupation of Iraq, 177,000 US service personnel were deployed there (Mockatis 2013). The United States controlled most Iraqi governments and was responsible for designating Iraq's prime minister for many years. The first of these, Ayad Allawi, was a CIA man (Claude 2004). Ibrahim al-Jaafari, the second prime minister, was elected by the transitional Iraqi National Assembly at the suggestion of viceroy Paul Bremer (Arnold and Wiener 2016: 397). The third prime minister, Nuri al-Maliki, was selected on the United States' recommendation (IBP 2013: 88). The fourth was Haidar Abadi, a prime minister very hostile to Iran and close to the United States who declared he would abide by the US sanctions on Iran (Goran 2018). Notwithstanding the US control over Iraq since 2003 and the presence of tens of thousands of troops, the United States has failed to win the hearts and minds of the population.

In an extraordinary session on Sunday the 5th of January, two days after a US drone strike on the convoy at Baghdad airport killing Soleimani and Muhandis, the Iraqi parliament voted for the departure of all foreign forces from the country (Magnier 2020). However, President Trump had no intention of leaving, and threatened to impose harsh sanctions if not allowed to keep his forces in the country (Gilsiman 2020). More conflicts and battles between the United States forces and Iraqi groups cannot be excluded in the future, contributing further to Iraq's destabilization.

Middle East, Asia Minor, India and Pakistan. When Alexander the Great conquered most of the empire in the fourth century BCE, it was a mixture of Persian and eastern Mediterranean cultures that created the Hellenistic Age. The last ancient kingdom was the Sassanian empire in the third century AD, which observed the rise of Buddhism, Zoroastrian, Judaism, Christianity and Islam. All these kingdoms and religions left behind a gigantic heritage for the modern world. Iran has an unparalleled twenty-two cultural sites on the UNESCO World Heritage list and many other ancient rich and noble sites expressing the grandeur of poetry, philosophy, architecture and science, including the shockingly beautiful ninth-century Masjed-e Jamé in Isfahan and the ancient Persian ruins of Persepolis, to name but a few.

1.2 Destabilizing Syria

At the beginning of the war in Syria in 2011, the world thought Syrian President Bashar al-Assad would be overthrown quickly. In 2012, the CIA, Saudi Arabia and Qatar financed more than 160 military cargos to be distributed to the opponents of the central government in Damascus (Chivers and Schmitt 2013). Jordan and Turkey offered free transit for weapons and jihadists. The presence of al-Qaeda was suddenly tolerated in Syria. All of this took place before the jihadists and rebels reached Aleppo, where life was still calm until mid-2012 when the devastating war then hit the entire country.

In two years, Qatar invested 3 billion US dollars to support jihadists and rebels in Syria (Khalaf and Fielding Smith 2013). 'Anything that went [to Syria], went to Turkey and was coordinated with US forces. [...] All distribution was done through the US and the Turks and us and everyone else that was involved', said former prime minister of Qatar Hamad bin Jassim bin Jaber al-Thani. Qatar's prime minister would, in fact, have liked for his government to end its support for jihadists such as Jabhat al-Nusra (Middle East Eye 2017).

Jabhat al-Nusra commander Abu Mohamad al-Joulani was sent by ISIS leader Abu Bakr al-Baghdadi to Syria in mid-2011 to prepare the ground for the 'Islamic State' in the Levant[5] (Anzalone 2016). The jihadist group Jabhat al-Nusra started to organize itself to build a strong recruitment network, aiming to establish an Islamic Caliphate in the Levant before expanding to other nearby Middle Eastern states.

The usual tactic of most religious non-state actors is to finance and send a large number of clerics into a new country as avant-garde messengers to prepare the ground for recruitment in the name of Islam. The deployment of these clerics targets mainly, but not exclusively, remote rural areas where large parts of the population are spread out, are less intellectuals and have little access to the outside world or to the cities. Individuals in remote areas are the most vulnerable to Islamic preaching. They were the first to join, motivated by (relatively) handsome financial rewards and religious arguments about stories reflecting the ancient battles and expansion of Islam and what to expect in the afterlife.

Two years after the beginning of the war, al-Joulani denounced his own commander (ISIS leader al-Baghdadi), joined al-Qaeda Central (2013) and ended up rebranding his group and taking a distance from al-Qaeda Central commander Ayman al-Zawahiri. He has kept thousands of foreign fighters (Tajik, Turkmen,

5 The Levant or Sham or *bilad al-Sham* in Arabic.

Uighur and many Arab, African and other nationals) embedded within his group under his command and renamed his group as Hayat Tahrir al-Sham (Zartman 2020: 120), to remain under the radar and avoid embarrassing his western, Arab and Turkish supporters. His new group – which espouses the same creed as ISIS and al-Qaeda but employs different tactics and priorities – was still, in March 2020, in total control of the northern Syrian city of Idlib where the Turkish forces of Ankara are deployed.

Al-Joulani believes in *al-Tamkeen* (empowerment). It consists in consolidating the group in the country (Syria) where it operates without necessarily expose the ultimate goal as al-Qaeda under Osama bin Laden did by declaring the 'far enemy' (the United States) as the main objective to its terrorist attacks. By keeping a domestic objective (overthrow President Bashar al-Assad), al-Joulani hopes to blurb the western countries' radar, join the western objective to change the regime in Syria, and lower the world' attention while his terrorist group is growing and expanding, if the opportunity arises. The jihadist leader established himself in his stronghold, the city of Idlib.

US counterterrorism officials have voiced concern (Wilson 2020) about thousands of al-Qaeda members who have adopted a new name, Hurras al-Din (Schmitt 2019). Due to the presence of hundreds of thousands of Syrian refugees in the city, the Syrian government was warned not to advance towards Idlib to liberate it (Trump 2018) notwithstanding the intensive gathering of jihadists. Yet, Brett McGurk, the former special presidential envoy for the Global Coalition to Defeat ISIS at the US Department of State and senior national security advisor under presidents George W. Bush and Barack Obama, described the city of Idlib as the 'largest al Qaeda safe haven since 9/11, tied directly to Ayman al-Zawahiri', the current leader of al-Qaeda who replaced Osama bin Laden (MEI 2017). It is a real challenge to find a balance between eliminating al-Qaeda and other jihadists and protecting, unscathed, hundreds of thousands of civilians in Idlib.

Al-Qaeda in Syria – which hosted some of the most wanted militants from all over the world (Doornbos and Moussa 2016) – and all the other jihadists fighting under different banners, were no longer perceived as the real enemy of the West. That approach was due to what was considered some form of pragmatism, even though the same al-Qaeda was responsible for the 9/11 terrorist attack (Gartenstein-Ross and Koduvayur 2019). In fact, to the world, President Assad and Iran were the real enemies. In reality, it was the regime-change objective driving media and western politicians who wanted the removal of President Bashar al-Assad that transformed jihadists into tolerated militants.

For that same purpose, the United States has secretly provided arms and training for Syrian jihadists and rebels since 2012 (Cloud and Abdulrahim 2013).

In 2015, US President Barack Obama acknowledged the failure of the country's 500 million US dollar campaign to train thirty fighters (al-Hamza brigade), who joined al-Qaeda in Syria, taking their US-manufactured weapons with them (Shear et al. 2015). In 2017, CIA Director Mike Pompeo recommended that President Trump shut down a 1 billion US dollar training programme, acknowledging that CIA-supplied weapons had ended up in the hands of al-Qaeda in Syria (Mazzetti et al. 2017). In four years, the US military and civilian investment in Syria to overthrow the Syrian government reached 12 billion US dollars (Ford 2018).

The United States, the Arab countries and Turkey were not the only regime-change players in Syria. Israeli Defence Minister Moshe Yaalon made explicit the country's preference to have ISIS on its borders rather than Iran (Moore 2016). Israel's Chief of Staff Lieutenant General Gadi Eisenkot admitted that Israel had lied about its non-intervention in the Syrian war and, on the record, confirmed it had armed Syrian militants in the Golan Heights to fight against the central government in Damascus (Levy 2019).

Israel has carried out hundreds of attacks on Syrian territory, benefiting from the presence of a friendly superpower (the United States) ready to intervene in case the Syrian government and its allies decide to retaliate (Kershner 2019). Israel has said it is fighting against Iran in Syria, but in fact it has been depleting the Syrian Army's capabilities, to prevent it eventually reclaiming the occupied Golan Heights. Israel believes the US presence in the Levant might deter Syria and its allies from fighting back against Israel's continuous bombing of their military assets. Hundreds of Syrian weapons warehouses have been destroyed by Israel. However, Syria and its allies seem to have found strength in this war, notwithstanding its devastating effect on the local population and the infrastructure of the country.

In 2017, the United Nations estimated the cost of rebuilding Syria's infrastructure at 250 billion US dollars (De Mistura 2017). The cost is most likely much higher, as the war continues in the north. Since 2011, Arab and western countries have invested billions of dollars in toppling President Assad, resulting in 400,000 deaths among the Syrian Army, the jihadists, the rebels and civilians, with many more wounded. Over six million refugees were internally displaced,[6] and 5.5 million refugees fled the country, mainly to Turkey, Lebanon, Jordan, Iraq and Egypt.[7] It was unclear what alternative (al-Qaeda and ISIS were by

---

6 See UNHCR website: *Syria – Protection*, https://www.unhcr.org/sy/protection.

7 See UNHCR Operational Portal: *Syria Regional Refugee Response*, https://data2.unhcr.org/en/situations/syria.

far the most powerful groups in the Syrian anti-Assad camp) the world had to offer to secularists, Druse, Christians, Alevi, Ismail's Twelvers, Kurds, Turkmen, Yazidi, Jews and non-violent Sunni Syrians.

It is rare for the west to successfully trigger a regime-change in the Middle East, and without unintended consequences. The 1982 Israeli invasion to Lebanon with the objective to expel the Palestine Liberation Organization gave birth to the Lebanese Hezbollah (Azani 2009: 241). The long years of war in Syria have boosted the military capability and skills of the Lebanese quasi-state actor Hezbollah and brought thousands of Iranian officers to the Levant to stay. The Syrian government asked its allies – Hezbollah, Iran and Russia – for help in fighting the jihadists and rebels financed by the United States, nearby Arab countries and Israel. The war has turned to the benefit of the central government with the defeat of ISIS.

President Assad remains in power, and Iran has established a strong base in Syria. Russia provided significant help in defeating the jihadists, enlarged its Mediterranean naval base in the coastal city of Tartous, established a military airport base in Khmeimim (also written Hmeimim, located south-east of the coastal city of Latakia in Latakia governorate) and consolidated its presence in the Levant. Russia is offering an alternative to US hegemony in the Middle East. It is not yet clear whether its behaviour will change once the war in Syria will be over, the entire Syrian territory is recovered under the central government in Damascus and Russia has a monopoly of control in the Levant.

US forces established a powerful military presence and several bases in the north-east of Syria under the UN mandate to fight terrorism (ISIS). The Syrian Army and its allies defeated ISIS in every city and rural area they reached, but they were stopped and prevented from crossing the Euphrates river to complete their mission and liberate the country. The United States, along with the local Syrian Kurds, fought against ISIS in the north-east and defeated the group. That should have meant the end of the US presence in Syria, which had been justified by the need to fight terrorism.

However, President Trump, who believed Syria to be a land of 'sand and death' (Marcin 2019), said he would stay 'only for the oil' (Borger 2019). President Trump seems comfortable with 'pillaging Syria's oil', considering the act as justified (Wright 2019). By taking this stand, President Trump has totally disavowed the Lieber Code, the Brussels Declaration, the Oxford Manual, the Hague convention,[8] the Charter of the Nuremberg International Military Tribunal

8 See UNESCO website: *1954 Hague Convention for the Protection of Cultural Property in the Event of Armed Conflict*, http://www.unesco.org/new/en/culture/themes/armed-conflict-and-heritage/convention-and-protocols/1954-hague-convention.

established after the Second World War and Article 53 of the Additional Protocol I to the Geneva Conventions prohibiting pillaging,[9] which under the statute of the International Criminal Court constitutes a war crime in international armed conflict.[10]

US four-star General Barry McCaffrey, who commanded a US Army division in Iraq, was surprised at what the United States had become. 'What are we becoming . . . pirates? If ISIS is defeated we lack Congressional authority to stay. The oil belongs to Syria' (Wright 2019). Legally, UN resolutions do not allow the United States to stay in Syria for the oil. President Trump has also alleged the right of Turkey to occupy more of Syria's territory (Schmitt et al. 2019) and prevented the Syrian Kurds from falling back to their government in Damascus (Dickey and Ackerman 2019).

However, President Trump has also said that he 'doesn't need Middle East oil' (Egan 2020). Moreover, the production of oil in north-east Syria is actually insignificant for the US economy. Therefore, the reason should be looked for somewhere else: to finance the Kurdish separatist forces who are operating as US proxies and wish to establish their own independent state. It seems to be irrelevant that the Kurdish People's Protection Units (YPG) are the Syrian branch of the Kurdistan Workers' Party (PKK), officially considered a terrorist group by the United States, the European Union (Roth and Sever 2006; Barnard and Hubbard 2018) and Turkey. The United States is no longer in a position to offer the Syrian Kurds the independent state they have long wished for (Yüksel and van Veen 2019) due to the Turkish intervention along the borders with Syria. The United States may also wish to stay in Syria in order to protect Israel, and to prevent the recovery of the Syrian economy.

Moreover, the United States has positioned its forces on the border crossing with Iraq at al-Tanf to stop the exchange of merchandise, the transit of business between the two countries and the flow of weapons from Tehran to Baghdad, Damascus and then Beirut to the Lebanese Hezbollah. The flow of weapons to Hezbollah has never ceased since 1982, including during the nine years of war in Syria. The Syrian war and Hezbollah's participation in it opened new avenues for the quasi-state actor to establish its own border crossing between Syria and Lebanon. Thus, closing the Tehran–Beirut road via al-Tanf will have little effect

---

9 See Customary IHL Database: *Protection of Cultural Objects and of Places of Worship*, https://ihl-databases.icrc.org/applic/ihl/ihl.nsf/WebART/470-750068.

10 See Customary IHL Database: *Rule 52. Pillage*, https://ihl-databases.icrc.org/customary-ihl/eng/docs/v1_rul_rule52.

on the supply of weapons to Hezbollah but a major consequence on the Syrian economy. Moreover, the Syrian–Iraqi crossing of al-Qaem has been reopened, providing an alternative route for Iran to support its allies, if and when needed. Al-Qaem crossing is still considered unsafe for civilian travelling between Iraq and Syria and I have been personally under ISIS attack during my latest journey on this specific road in the month of February 2020. ISIS remnants are still operating a hit-and-run tactics in this remote area, spread over the deserted area between Tadmur (Palmyra) and al-Qaem.

The Syrian government is gaining momentum on the battlefield and spreading its control over larger parts of the country. Arab Gulf countries have tempered their initial enthusiasm for reopening their embassies and becoming involved in the reconstruction of Syria, cost estimated to be almost 400 billion US dollars (Barnes-Dacey 2019: 60). Jordan has limited the transit of Syrian merchandise through its territory to the Arab countries. If this trade were unrestricted, it could provide substantial support to the Syrian economy. Europe and the United States are still imposing sanctions, and are manifestly not convinced to allow the Syrian government to boost its economy and restore the country to its 2010 conditions.

The Syrian population suffers profoundly, not only from the consequences of many years of war, but also from international sanctions. The primary source of energy (gas and oil) and grain in north-east Syria is under US and Turkish occupation and control. The devaluation of the local currency is adding more pressure to Syrian daily life. This situation has contributed to the instability of the Levant and fuelled the migration of its population towards better opportunities when available in nearby countries.

The Syrian government continues to pursue the liberation of the northern part of the country, but in the newly liberated region I was eyewitness to a troubling discovery. The content of the Hill of Mardikh, known as Ebla (Etheredge 2011: 7), south of the northern city of Saraqeb, has been damaged and is in a perilous state. This Bronze Age site, dates to the third millennium BCE, provided new perspectives on the Syrian civilization. Jihadists destroyed all the artefacts that were previously carefully stored and drove their tanks into the walls and the rooms of the site. Sadly, this is nothing new for Syria, where jihadists, from ISIS to al-Qaeda and the other rebranded jihadists who control the north today, all have done their best to wipe out the traces of preceding ancient civilizations.

Syria did not fall to the violent extremists, though the jihadists took their revenge by destroying much of the ancient history of the Levant. The destruction of the ancient city of Palmyra by ISIS was devastating. The city, which I visited in February 2020, is almost abandoned. The Syrian steppe offers a perfect shelter to these jihadists on the run. There will be little hope for the rebirth of the Syrian cultural heritage unless and until total stability is restored in Syria.

Syria needs national reconciliation, the withdrawal of all foreign forces and a reconstruction plan to keep its inhabitants in place and help overcome the consequences of war. There always seems to be little money available to finance reconstruction and prosperity, compared with the chilling amounts that are spent on wars. The Watson Institute estimates the cost of the 'war on terror' to be 6.4 trillion US dollars (Crawford 2019) – an amount that could have put an end to poverty in the Middle East.

Conclusion

The situation in Iraq remains volatile. Its government has little hope of becoming effective and has failed to understand its responsibilities since at least the Iraq war. Iraqi politicians have not learned to serve the population. They have been engaged frenetically in corruption activities, neglecting the country's basic needs to rebuild the infrastructure, offer job opportunities and reach national reconciliation. Good governance is an essential prerequisite for stability and for the well-being of the population.

In its pursuit of stability, Iraq has not been able to find a way to construct the alliances it needs. The country is trapped between mandatory domestic reforms and a balance between the strategic relationship with the United States and the inseparable relationship with its neighbour Iran, with whom it has its longest borders and a religious bond. The United States has no apparent plan for Iraq and, in a similar way to Iran, has failed to understand the culture or even figure out how to deal with the Iraqis. Many mistakes have been made on both sides. However, Iran has managed to secure some support from non-state actors, while the United States has failed to demonstrate a consistent policy and secure allies.

All options available at the moment are not great for the stability of Iraq. If the United States succeeds in reshuffling its policy and reconstructing its relationship with Iraq, it may have some chance of success if it takes a different approach from the current one. Maintaining a military force in the country does not provide an additional advantage to the United States; on the contrary, US forces are at the moment potential targets. Unless the US–Iran tension is eased, stability is not around the corner.

Finally, notwithstanding the defeat of ISIS and its dis-location from all cities and villages, the group is still present. If fertile ground is available – and it certainly is not lacking – the group will have more chances to return. ISIS remnants are a constant threat, capable of hit-and-run insurgency all over the country.

Therefore, Iraq will find it more difficult to look after its cultural heritage in remote areas for fear of ISIS looking for soft targets. Only durable stability in Iraq will enable it to restore its peace and protect its World Heritage sites. If it ever manages to regain its full momentum, Iraq itself could potentially be the best line of defence against violent regional extremists.

In Syria, tens of thousands of foreign fighters were allowed to join al-Qaeda in order to destabilize the country, to establish an Islamic Caliphate or to transform the Levant into vast stateless chaos. Jihadists have created havoc with mass killings, and the oppression of human freedom of expression and worship. They have killed anyone who contradicts their extreme ideology and wiped out many ancient artefacts and sites. It is indeed the general practice of violent extremists to destroy everything and leave nothing behind. These jihadists destroyed invaluable ancient World Heritage sites and unique artefacts in Iraq and Syria. They are still fighting in Syria and threatening the stability of the country.

The Syrian government will want to free the entire country from all occupying forces. If the war continues, Syria will not have durable stability, and protecting cultural sites will not be among its priorities.

The cost of war and the destabilization of the Middle East – financed mainly by Middle Eastern assets – has touched millions of lives and cost trillions of dollars. A mere fragment of this bloody investment could have created prosperity for many generations to come. But the wealth of the Middle East was invested in its destruction. This part of the world contains humanity's richest cultural heritage. Given the forces that have been unleashed there, it needs to be carefully looked after and protected. This can only happen once all wars have ended, and in the Middle Eastern region this will not occur anytime soon.

References

Abu Rumman, Muhammad (2008), 'The Politics of Sunni Armed Groups in Iraq', in *Sada*, 18 August, https://carnegieendowment.org/sada/20836

Alkaff, Syed Huzaifah and Muhammad Haziq Bin Jani (2016), 'The Death of IS Top Strategist: Reflections on Counter-Terrorism Efforts', in *Counter Terrorist Trends and Analysis*, Vol. 8, No. 9, September, p. 4–9, https://www.rsis.edu.sg/rsis-publication/icpvtr/counter-terrorist-trends-and-analysis-ctta-volume-8-issue-09

Anzalone, Christopher (2016), 'The Multiple Faces of Jabhat al-Nusra/Jabhat Fath al-Sham in Syria's Civil War', in *Insight Turkey*, Vol. 18, No. 2, Spring, p. 41–51

Arango, Tim and Eric Schmitt (2014), 'U.S. Actions in Iraq Fueled Rise of a Rebel', in *The New York Times*, 10 August, https://nyti.ms/XbQ5e2

Arnold, James R. and Roberta Wiener, eds (2016), *Understanding U.S. Military Conflicts through Primary Sources. Vol. 4*, Santa Barbara, ABC-CLIO

Atwan, Abdel Bari (2015), *Islamic State. The Digital Caliphate*, Oakland, University of California Press

Azani, Eitan (2009), *Hezbollah: The Story of the Party of God. From Revolution to Institutionalization*, New York, Palgrave Macmillan

Bakawan, Adel (2017), 'Three generations of Jihadism in Iraqi Kurdistan', in Notes de l'Ifri, July, https://www.ifri.org/en/node/13243

Baker, Peter and Thomas Gibbons-Neff (2020), 'Esper Says He Saw No Evidence Iran Targeted 4 Embassies, as Story Shifts Again', in *The New York Times*, 12 January, https://nyti.ms/2R7cxCk

Barnard, Anne and Ben Hubbard (2018), 'Allies or Terrorists: Who Are the Kurdish Fighters in Syria?', in *The New York Times*, 25 January, https://nyti.ms/2GhgZrX

Barnard, Anne and Hwaida Saad (2015), 'Palmyra Temple Was Destroyed by ISIS, U.N. Confirms', in *The New York Times*, 31 August, https://nyti.ms/1EvjSTs

Barnes, Julian E. (2019), 'U.S. Launches Airstrikes on Iranian-Backed Forces in Iraq and Syria', in *The New York Times*, 29 December, https://nyti.ms/2MFISi9

Barnes-Dacey, Julien (2019), 'Geo-Politics of Reconstruction: Who Will Rebuild Syria and Pay for It?', in Eugenio Dacrema and Valeria Talbot, eds, *Rebuilding Syria. The Middle East's Next Power Game?*, Milan, Ledizioni, p. 59–73, https://www.ispionline.it/en/node/23863

Beauchamp, Zack (2015), 'Yes, Bush Helped Create ISIS – and Set Up the Middle East for a Generation of Chaos', in *Vox*, 2 June, https://www.vox.com/2015/6/2/8703059/bush-isis-middle-east

Biden, Joseph R. and Leslie H. Gelb (2006), 'Unity Through Autonomy in Iraq', in *The New York Times*, 1 May,https://www.nytimes.com/2006/05/01/opinion/01biden.html

Black, Elspeth (2017), 'The History and Importance of the Five Cities of Iraq', in *The Culture Trip*, 12 July, https://theculturetrip.com/middle-east/iraq/articles/the-five-holy-cities-of-iraq

Borger, Julian (2019), 'Trump Contradicts Aides and Says Troops in Syria "Only for Oil"', in *The Guardian*, 13 November, https://gu.com/p/cyh9m

Bori, Caterina (2004), 'A New Source for the Biography of Ibn Taymiyya', in *Bulletin of the School of Oriental and African Studies*, Vol. 67, No. 3, p. 321–348

Bowen, Jeremy (2020), 'Qasem Soleimani: Why His Killing Is Good News for IS Jihadists', in *BBC News*, 10 January, https://www.bbc.com/news/world-middle-east-51021861

Brzezinski, Zbigniew (1983), *Power and Principle: Memoirs of the National Security Adviser, 1977–1981*, New York, Farrar, Straus & Giroux

Bunzel, Cole (2015), 'From Paper State to Caliphate: The Ideology of the Islamic State', in *Brooking Project on U.S. Relations with the Islamic World Analysis Papers*, No. 19, March, http://brook.gs/2bjRKoa

Chamytelli, Maher and Isabel Coles (2016), 'Post-Islamic State Iraq Should Be Split in Three: Top Kurdish Official', in *Reuters*, 16 June, http://reut.rs/21nTrFe

Chivers, C.J. and Eric Schmitt (2013), 'Arms Airlift to Syria Rebels Expands, With Aid From C.I.A.', in *The New York Times*, 25 March, https://nyti.ms/32bLwSd

Chomsky, Noam (2008), 'Power and Globalization in the New World Order', in Henry Veltmeyer, ed. (2008), *New Perspectives on Globalization and Antiglobalization. Prospects for a New World Order?*, Aldershot/Burlington, Ashgate, p. 159–172

Chulov, Martin (2014), 'ISIS: The Inside Story', in *The Guardian*, 11 December, https://gu.com/p/4443c

Claude, Patrice (2004), 'The CIA Main Man in Baghdad', in *The Guardian*, 23 July, https://gu.com/p/hgt4

Cloud, David S. and Raja Abdulrahim (2013), 'U.S. Has Secretly Provided Arms Training to Syria Rebels Since 2012', in *Los Angeles Times*, 21 June, https://www.latimes.com/world/middleeast/la-xpm-2013-jun-21-la-fg-cia-syria-20130622-story.html

Coles, Isabel (2014), 'Iran Supplied Weapons to Iraqi Kurdish Forces; Baghdad Bomb Kills 12', in *Reuters*, http://reut.rs/1wwbHkF

Coles, Isabel (2020), 'Tens of Thousands March in Baghdad Against U.S. Troops in Iraq', in *The Wall Street Journal*, 24 January

Cooper, Helene (2007), 'Biden Plan for "Soft Partition" of Iraq Gains Momentum', in *The New York Times*, 30 July, https://www.nytimes.com/2007/07/30/world/americas/30iht-letter.1.6894357.html

Correll, Diana Stancy (2020), '109 US Troops Diagnosed with TBI After Iran Missile Barrage Sayed Pentagon in Latest Update', in *Military Times*, 10 February, https://www.militarytimes.com/news/your-military/2020/02/10/more-than-100-us-troops-diagnosed-with-tbi-after-irans-attack-at-al-asad-report

Crawford, Neta C. (2019), 'United States Budgetary Costs and Obligations of Post-9/11 Wars through FY2020: $6.4 Trillion', in *Costs of War Papers*, 13 November,https://watson.brown.edu/costsofwar/figures/2019/budgetary-costs-post-911-wars-through-fy2020-64-trillion

Daly, Michael (2017), 'ISIS Leader: "See You in New York"', in *Daily Beast*, 14 April, https://www.thedailybeast.com/isis-leader-see-you-in-new-york

Delanghe, Philippe (2008), 'May the Holy River Karun Mourn You (Gilgamesh VIII, 18): UNESCO's Post-Conflict Strategies for Safeguarding Cultural Heritage', in Peter G. Stone Joanne Farchakh Bajjaly, eds, *The Destruction of Cultural Heritage in Iraq*, Woodbridge, Boydell & Brewer, p. 193–200

De Mistura, Staffan (2017), *Security Council Briefing on the Situation in Syria*, 27 November, https://www.un.org/undpa/en/node/184102

Dickey, Christopher and Spencer Ackerman (2019), 'The U.S. Spoiled a Deal That Might Have Saved the Kurds, Former Top Official Says', in *Daily Beast*, 14 October, https://www.thedailybeast.com/the-us-spoiled-a-deal-that-might-have-saved-the-kurds-former-top-official-says

Doornbos, Harald and Jenan Moussa (2016), 'Present at the Creation', in *Foreign Policy*, 16 August

Egan, Matt (2020), 'Trump Says America Doesn't Need Middle East Oil. It's Not That Simple', in *CNN*, 8 January, https://edition.cnn.com/2020/01/08/business/oil-middle-east-trump-iran

Etheredge, Laura, ed. (2011), *Middle East Region in Transition. Historic Palestine, Israel, and the Emerging Palestinian Autonomous Areas*, New York, Britannica Educational Publishing

Fisk, Robert (1993), 'Anti-Soviet Warrior Puts His Army on the Road to Peace. . .', in *The Independent*, 6 December, https://www.independent.co.uk/news/world/anti-soviet-warrior-puts-his-army-on-the-road-to-peace-the-saudi-businessman-who-recruited-mujahedin-1465715.html

Flynn, Michael (2016), Transcript: Michael Flynn on ISIL, in *Al Jazeera*, 13 January, http://aje.io/ed94

Ford, Robert S. (2018), *Syria: Which Way Forward?*, Testimony before the House Foreign Affairs Committee, 6 February, http://docs.house.gov/meetings/FA/FA13/20180206/106832/HHRG-115-FA13-Wstate-FordR-20180206.pdf

Fuller, Graham E. and Rend Rahim Francke (2001), *The Arab Shi'a. The Forgotten Muslims*, New York, Palgrave Macmillan

Gartenstein-Ross, Daveed and Varsha Koduvayur (2019), 'How to Win Friends and Wage Jihad', in *Foreign Affairs*, 1 July

Gibbs, David N. (2000), 'Afghanistan: The Soviet Invasion in Retrospect', in *International Politics*, Vol. 37, No. 2, June, p. 233–246

Gilsiman, Kathy (2020), 'Iraq Is the One War Zone Trump Doesn't Want to Leave', in *The Atlantic*, 3 February, https://www.theatlantic.com/politics/archive/2020/02/trump-troops-iraq-iran-soleimani_isis/605908

Girardet, Edward (2011), *Killing the Cranes. A Reporter's Journey Through Three Decades of War in Afghanistan*, White River Junction, Chelsea Green Publishing

Gittleson, Ben (2020), '"Doesn't Really Matter": Trump On Whether Threat From Iranian General "Imminent"', in *ABC News*, 14 January, https://abcn.ws/2u01L8V

Goran, Baxtiyar (2018), 'Iraq Does Not Agree But Will Abide by US Sanctions on Iran: PM Abadi', in *Kurdistan 24*, 7 August, https://www.kurdistan24.net/en/news/ea6cb22c-c624-43d6-9e84-dbc56f2116a1

Goudsouzian, Tanya and Lara Fatah (2014), 'Analysis: The Kurds Take Kirkuk, Now What?', in *Al Jazeera*, 16 June,https://www.aljazeera.com/news/middleeast/2014/06/analysis-kurds-take-kirkuk-now-what-201461653255207327.html

Hamasaeed, Sarhang and Garrett Nada (2019), 'Iraq Timeline: Since the 2003 War', in *USIP Publications*, 9 July, https://www.usip.org/publications/2019/07/iraq-timeline-2003-war

Heing, Bridey (2018), *Cultural Destruction by ISIS*, New York, Enslow Publishing

Holmes, Oliver (2020), 'US and Allies on High Alert as Iran Threatens Retaliation', in *The Guardian*, 3 January, https://gu.com/p/d325k

Hubbard, Ben, Sebnem Arsu and Ceylan Yeginsu (2014), 'Turkey Obtains Release of Hostages Held in Iraq', in *The New York Times*, 20 September,https://www.nytimes.com/2014/09/21/world/middleeast/dozens-of-turkish-hostages-held-by-islamic-state-are-freed.html

IBP – International Business Publications (2013), *Iraq Country Study Guide. Vol. 1: Strategic Information and Developments*, Washington, International Business Publications

Jaffer, Kumail (2019), 'World War 3: Why Iran Could Be One of Seven Countries Trump Wants to "Take Out"', in *Express*, 21 June,https://www.express.co.uk/news/world/1143547

Jakes, Lara (2020), 'Defenders of History Take Aim at Trump's Threat to Strike Iran's Cultural Sites', in *The New York Times*, 5 January, https://nyti.ms/2QHSCJS

Kershner, Isabel (2019), 'Israel, in Rare Admission, Confirms Strike on Iranian Targets in Syria', in *The New York Times*, 13 January, https://nyti.ms/2QIHt9Z

Khalaf, Roula and Abigail Fielding Smith (2013), 'Qatar Bankrolls Syrian Revolt With Cash and Arms', in *The Financial Times*, 16 may, http://ig-legacy.ft.com/content/86e3f28e-be3a-11e2-bb35-00144feab7de

Kramer, Ronald, Raymond Michalowski and Dawn Rothe (2005), '"The Supreme International Crime". How the U.S. War in Iraq Threatens the Rule of Law', in *Social Justice*, Vol. 32, No. 2 (100), p. 52–81

Ledeen, Michael A. (2002), *The War Against the Terror Masters. Why it Happened, Where We Are Now, How We'll Win*, New York, Truman Talley Books

Levy, Daniel J. (2019), 'Israel Just Admitted Arming anti-Assad Syrian Rebels. Big Mistake', in *Haaretz*, 3 February, https://www.haaretz.com/israel-news/.premium-israel-just-admitted-arming-anti-assad-syrian-rebels-big-mistake-1.6894850

Lister, Tim and Eve Brower (2020), 'Growing Doubts on Legality of US Strike That Killed Iranian General', in *CNN*, 6 January,https://edition.cnn.com/2020/01/06/middleeast/soleimani-strike-legality-doubts-us-iran-intl

MacDonald, David B., Dirk Nabers, Robert G. Patman, eds (2012), *The Bush Leadership, the Power of Ideas, and the War on Terror*, London/New York, Routledge

Magnier, Elijah J. (2018), 'Who Boosted Qassem Soleimani's Image and Spread Iran's Influence Throughout the Middle East', in *Middle East Politics*, 27 November, https://wp.me/p47Jgd-1by

Magnier, Elijah J. (2019a), 'Iran and Trump on the Edge of the Abyss', in *Middle East Politics*, 21 June, https://wp.me/p47Jgd-1Fb

Magnier, Elijah J. (2019b), 'The US and Iran in Iraq: Protestors Take Over the Streets, Demanding Government Reforms "Or Else"', in *Middle East Politics*, 17 November, https://wp.me/p47Jgd-1ZA

Magnier, Elijah J. (2019c), 'Why Didn't Iraq Retaliate Against Israel? Part 1–2', in *Middle East Politics*, 21 September, https://ejmagnier.com/2019/09/21/why-didnt-iraq-retaliate-against-israel-part-1-2

Magnier, Elijah J. (2020), 'Immediate US Withdrawal Due to Its Violation of the Agreement and Iraq Sovereignty', in *Middle East Politics*, 22 January, https://wp.me/p47Jgd-2dq

Marcin, Tim (2019), 'Donald Trump Calls Syria "Sand and Death," Says "We're Not Talking About Vast Wealth"', in *Newsweek*, 2 January, https://www.newsweek.com/donald-trump-syria-sand-death-1277413

Mazzetti, Mark, Adam Goldman and Michael S. Schmidt (2017), 'Behind the Sudden Death of a $1 Billion Secret C.I.A. War in Syria', in *The New York Times*, 2 August, http://nyti.ms/2u60Dfv

McCoy, Terrence (2014), 'Camp Bucca: The US Prison That Became the Birthplace of ISIS', in *The Independent*, 4 November,https://www.independent.co.uk/news/world/middle-east/camp-bucca-the-us-prison-that-became-the-birthplace-of-isis-9838905.html

MEI – Middle East Institute (2017), *Assessing the Trump Administration's Counterterrorism Policy* (video), 27 July, http://education.mei.edu/node/25735

Michael, George (2007), 'The Legend and Legacy of Abu Musab al-Zarqawi', in *Defence Studies*, Vol. 7, No. 3, September, p. 338–357

Middle East Eye (2017), 'Qatar "Maybe" Supported al-Qaeda in Syria, Says Former PM', in *Middle East Eye*, 31 October, https://www.middleeasteye.net/node/66993

Mockatis, Thomas R. (2013), *The Iraq War Encyclopaedia*, Santa Barbara, California ABC-Clio

Mogelson, Luke (2016), 'The Front Lines', in *The New Yorker*, 18 January, https://www.newyorker.com/magazine/2016/01/18/the-front-lines

Moore, Jack (2016), 'Israeli Defense Minister: I Prefer ISIS to Iran on Our Borders', in *Newsweek*, 20 January, https://www.newsweek.com/israeli-defense-minister-i-prefer-isis-iran-our-borders-417726

Mortimer, Caroline (2017), 'CIA Officer Who Interrogated Saddam Hussein Says There Were Clearly No WMDs in Iraq', in *The Independent*, 4 January, https://www.independent.co.uk/news/world/middle-east/cia-officer-saddam-hussein-interrogate-wmds-iraq-weapons-of-mass-destruction-war-a7509081.html

Oweis, Khaled Yacoub Oweis (2020), 'Ali Al Sistani: The Subtle Ayatollah Shaping Politics in Baghdad', in *The National*, 1 January, https://www.thenational.ae/world/mena/ali-al-sistani-the-subtle-ayatollah-shaping-politics-in-baghdad-1.958716

Parker, Ned, Isabel Coles and Raheem Salman (2014), 'Special Report: How Mosul Fell – An Iraqi General Disputes Baghdad's Story', in *Reuters*, 14 October,http://reut.rs/1xNKOFK

Rawaf, Salman (2013), 'The 2003 Iraq War and Avoidable Death Toll', in *PLoS Medicine*, Vol. 10, No. 10, October, art. e1001533, https://doi.org/10.1371/journal.pmed.1001532

Roggio, Bill and Amir Toumaj (2016), 'Qods Force Commander An Official Advisor to Government, Iraq's Foreign Minister Says', in *Long War Journal*, 7 June, https://www.longwarjournal.org/archives/2016/06/

qods-force-commander-an-official-advisor-to-government-iraqs-foreign-minister-says.php

Rosemberg, Elizabeth (2019), 'Maximum Pressure on Iran Won't Work', in *Foreign Policy*, 26 April, https://foreignpolicy.com/2019/04/26/maximum-pressure-on-iran-wont-work

Roth, Mitchel P. and Murat Sever (2006), 'The Kurdish Workers Party (PKK) as Criminal Syndicate: Finding terrorism Through Organised Crime, A Case Study', in *Studies in Conflict & Terrorism*, Vol. 30, No. 10, p. 901–920

Rubin, Alissa J. (2020), 'Was U.S. Wrong About Attack That Nearly Started a War With Iran?', in *The New York Times*, 6 February, https://nyti.ms/2H55OUJ

Rubin, Alissa J. and Ronen Bergman (2019), 'Israeli Airstrike Hits Weapons Depot in Iraq', in *The New York Times*, 22 August, https://nyti.ms/2HneG8V

Schmitt, Eric (2015), 'Iran Sent Arms to Iraq to Fight ISIS, U.S. Says', in *The New York Times*, 16 March, https://nyti.ms/1DutwE5

Schmitt, Eric (2019), 'U.S. Sees Rising Threat in the West From Qaeda Branch in Syria', in *The New York Times*, 29 September, https://nyti.ms/2m99z4V

Schmitt, Eric, Maggie Haberman and Edward Wong (2019), 'President Endorses Turkish Military Operation in Syria, Shifting U.S. Policy', in *The New York Times*, 8 October,https://nyti.ms/2obcMSC

Shafaaq (2014), 'Hashemi Congratulates the Fall of Mosul, Describe It as "Revolution of the Oppressed"', in *Shafaq News*, 11 June, https://www.shafaaq.com/en/iraq-news/hashemi-congratulates-the-fall-of-mosul-describe-it-as-revolution-of-the-oppressed

Shear, Michael, Helene Cooper and Eric Schmitt (2015), 'Obama Administration Ends Effort to Train Syrians to Combat ISIS', in *The New York Times*, 9 October, https://www.nytimes.com/2015/10/10/world/middleeast/pentagon-program-islamic-state-syria.html

Strachan, Anna Louise (2017), 'Factors Behind the Fall of Mosul to ISIL (Daesh) in 2014', in *K4D Helpdesk Reports*, 17 January, https://opendocs.ids.ac.uk/opendocs/handle/20.500.12413/13051

Strick van Linschoten, Alex and Felix Kuehn, eds (2018), *The Taliban Reader. War, Islam and Politics*, Oxford, Oxford University Press

Times of Israel (2020), 'Iraqi PM: US Told Us Israel Bombed Prop-Iran Militias in Iraq Last Summer', in *The Times of Israel*, 5 January, https://www.timesofisrael.com/iraqi-pm-us-said-israel-bombed-pro-iran-militias-in-iraq

Trump, Donald J. (2018), [@realDonaldTrump] 'President Bashar al-Assad of Syria must not recklessly attack Idlib Province. . .', in *Twitter*, 4 September,https://twitter.com/realDonaldTrump/status/1036740691211284480

UNESCO (2015), *UNESCO Alarmed by News of Mass Destruction of Books in Mosul*, 3 February, https://en.unesco.org/node/239792

US Congress (2010), *Hearings before a Subcommittee of the Committee on Appropriations, House of Representatives . . . Part 5-State, Foreign Operations, and Related Programs Appropriations for 2010*, 55–951, Washington, U.S. Government Printing Office, https://www.govinfo.gov/content/pkg/CHRG-111hhrg55951/html/CHRG-111hhrg55951.htm

Uskowi, Nader (2019), *Temperature Rising. Iran's Revolutionary Guards and Wars in the Middle East*, Lanham, Rowan & Littlefield

Verini, James (2019), *They Will Have to Die Now. Mosul and the Fall of the Caliphate*, New York, W.W. Norton & Company

Whiteside, Craig (2015), 'Mosul: A Bridge Too Far?', in *War on the Rocks*, 18 March, https://warontherocks.com/?p=7620

Whiteside, Craig (2017), 'A Pedigree of Terror: The Myth of Ba'athist Influence in the Islamic State Movement', in *Perspectives on Terrorism*, Vol. 11, No. 3, June, http://www.terrorismanalysts.com/pt/index.php/pot/article/view/605

Wilson, Audrey (2020), 'United States Issues Warning to Russia Over Syria Policy', in *Foreign Policy*, 6 February

Worley, Will (2016), 'ISIS Destroys Gates to Ancient City of Nineveh Near Mosul', in *The Independent*, 12 April, https://www.independent.co.uk/news/world/middle-east/isis-destroys-gates-ancient-city-nineveh-mosul-a6980686.html

Wright, Robin (2019), 'Trump's Baffling Plan to Pillage Syria's Oil', in *The New Yorker*, 30 October, https://www.newyorker.com/news/our-columnists/trumps-baffling-plan-to-pillage-syrias-oil

Wyndham, Constance (2015, p. 122), 'Reconstructing Afghan Identity: Nation-Building, International Relations and the Safeguarding of Afghanistan's Buddhist Heritage', in Paul Basu and Wayne Modest, eds, *Museums, Heritage and International Development*, New York/London, Routledge, p. 122–142

Yeung, Peter (2020), 'Leading Art Institutions Denounce President Trump's Threats to Destroy Iranian Cultural Heritage', in *Architectural Digest*, 7 January,https://www.architecturaldigest.com/story/the-met-president-trumps-threats-destroy-iranian-cultural-heritage

Yüksel, Engin & Erwin van Veen (2019), 'Turkey in Northwestern Syria. Rebuilding Empire at the Margins', in *Clingendael CRU Policy Briefs*, June, https://www.clingendael.org/node/10327

Zarkawi, Abu Musab (2004), *Zarqawi Letter. February 2004 Coalition Provisional Authority English translation of terrorist Musab al Zarqawi letter obtained by United States Government in Iraq*, https://2001-2009.state.gov/p/nea/rls/31694.htm

Zartman, Jonathan K., ed. (2020), *Conflict in the Modern Middle East. An Encyclopedia of Civil War, Revolutions, and Regime Change*, Santa Barbara, ABC-CLIO

Francesco Bandarin

Chapter 2: The Reconstruction and Recovery of Syrian Cultural Heritage: The Case of the Old City of Aleppo

Eight years of conflict have severely disrupted the fabric of Syrian society and its economy and have created a humanitarian crisis of unprecedented proportions. According to the United Nations (UN), an estimated 11.7 million people needed humanitarian assistance at the end of 2018, with about 6.2 million still internally displaced, and over 5 million refugees residing in other countries.[1]

All the major cities of the country have suffered devastating damage: from Damascus (albeit not in its historic centre), to Aleppo, Homs, Hama, Raqqa and Deir er-Zor, the urban landscape is dominated by the ruins of housing structures, public and private buildings, monuments, mosques, churches and infrastructure. Many other medium-size and small settlements have been heavily damaged and have lost all or part of their population (REACH and UNITAR 2019).

All the rich heritage sites of Syria, and in particular its World Heritage sites, have suffered massive damage, including Palmyra, where the Islamic State of Iraq and Syria (ISIS) demolished the major ancient temples of Bel and Baalshamin with explosives; the Crac des Chevaliers, one of the most important citadels of the Crusades era; the Dead Cities of northern Syria, an important site for religious life during the Byzantine period; Bosra, the ancient capital of the Roman province of Arabia; the monument areas of Aleppo; and, to a lesser extent, the historic centre of Damascus. Several other sites of great historical and artistic significance, including Apamea, Ebla and Mari, among others, have been pillaged and plundered by treasure hunters, causing enormous damage to their archaeological value.

The conflict ravaged the City of Aleppo during four long years (2012–16). During this time, the central areas of the historic city, where the most important monuments are located, were the scene of heavy fighting and attacks that obliterated many significant historical buildings and left several others in a state of

1 Since the outbreak of the crisis in 2011, Syria has dropped in the Human Development Index from 113 to 173 out of 187 countries, placing Syria in the bottom tenth percentile globally.

Figure 2.1: Destruction of the Old City of Aleppo, situation in November 2010 and October 2014.
Source: Awford (2014).[2]

partial or complete destruction (Figure 2.1). Reconstructing and restoring the Ancient City of Aleppo will be a major challenge in the years to come, one that will require significant technical and financial resources.

However, the current international political situation, characterized by a polarized attitude towards the Syrian government, with most western countries supporting sanctions that preclude the transfer of aid and financial support for the reconstruction of the country, constitutes a major obstacle to attempts to kick-start the reconstruction process and to restore the country's world-class heritage. In the nearly three years since the Syrian government regained control of the City of Aleppo, only limited interventions have been carried out, supported in part by national and local institutions, and in part by international organizations. Some of the initial efforts have been directed at clearing the debris of collapsed buildings, repairing the buildings and monuments that suffered less serious damage, protecting the existing cultural heritage from further damage and depletion, and organizing the technical and operational systems needed for the reconstruction process.

The economy of the city has also suffered from the protracted conflict. In particular, its centuries-old markets, once considered one of the wonders of the Middle East, endured major destruction and disruption, and largely remain

2 See also UNESCO website: *Gallery: Heritage at Risk in Syria*, https://en.unesco.org/photo-galleries/26413.

non-operational. Given the strategic importance of this economic infrastructure for the rebirth of the city, special attention has been given to its restoration and rehabilitation, through model restoration projects and some initial rehabilitation activities. Regenerating the economy of Aleppo, historically one of the most active and vibrant cities of the entire region, will be fundamental to allow thousands of families to return to their homes and their livelihoods. However, the current level of effort is insufficient to ensure a speedy post-conflict recovery process.

In spite of the difficulties of the current political environment, attempts have been made to establish a medium- and long-term strategy for the reconstruction and recovery of the city, as expressed in the document 'Vision and Planning Framework', recently submitted to the UNESCO World Heritage Committee (DGAM 2019a).[3]

2.1 Previous initiatives (1990–2011)

In the decades before the crisis, major international co-operation projects were implemented in the Ancient City of Aleppo under the umbrella of co-operation initiatives between the local government and international public and private organizations (Bianca et al. 1980).[4] Major partners in these activities included the German Development Agency (GTZ, now GIZ) and the Arab Fund for Economic and Social Development. During the period 1992–2010, the Aleppo Urban Development Project addressed the rebuilding of streets and the upgrading of many city services (such as the sewage system), as well as the restoration of hundreds of houses in the historic Old City (Stürzbecher et al. 1998). The comprehensive GTZ project (DOC and GTZ 1998, 2005; Saad and Stellmach 2010), implemented in collaboration with the Aga Khan Trust for Culture (AKTC), included: (a) reorganization of the traffic in and around the

3 The document was prepared by the Directorate-General of Antiquities and Museums in co-operation with the Aga Khan Trust for Culture and presented to UNESCO and to the 43rd session of the World Heritage Committee, Baku, July 2019. Part of the information presented in this chapter is derived from this document.

4 In 1992, the Project for the Rehabilitation of Old Aleppo was set up under the Municipality of Aleppo in co-operation with international agencies. In 1999, the Directorate of the Old City was established under the Municipality of Aleppo to guide the rehabilitation of the Old City, with three departments covering studies and planning, permits and monitoring, and implementation and maintenance.

Citadel area; (b) management of the commercial and tourism sectors; (c) protection of the residential areas; (d) support for cultural functions and rehabilitation efforts; and (e) improvement of public spaces (Jodido 2011).

The Directorate-General of Antiquities and Museums (DGAM) between 2000 and 2008 took responsibility, jointly with the AKTC, for a comprehensive campaign for the restoration of the Citadel of Aleppo. The main objectives of this project comprised: (a) reorientation of the traffic in and around the Citadel area and the creation of pedestrian spaces; (b) the building of public transport networks and parking areas; (c) protection of the physical and historical environment of the Citadel perimeter; (d) control of the expansion of the commercial sector; and (e) improvement of public spaces, infrastructure elements, landscaping, pavements and lighting. By 2011, at the end of a thirty-year cycle of interventions, all of Aleppo's monuments had been restored and all of the public spaces of the inner city had been rehabilitated.

2.2 Aleppo at war, 2012–2016

Four years of intensive fighting between government and opposition forces have left the Old City of Aleppo in ruins. According to reports by the World Bank (2017) and UN-Habitat (2014), out of a population of around 3 million inhabitants in 2011, by 2014 more than 900,000 were displaced outside and more than 800,000 inside the city. This was due to the massive destruction of urban housing resulting from the conflict, affecting over 30,000 housing units (Figure 2.2), paralleled by widespread disruption of the city's infrastructure, social and health services, educational facilities and economic activities. For four years, water and electricity were unavailable or available only in very limited quantities. Beginning in 2014, a new cycle of escalation further worsened an already critical situation: during the following two years, until the end of the conflict in 2016, the city infrastructure suffered severe damage (Figure 2.3).

While serious damage was widespread and practically no areas of the city escaped unscathed, the greatest devastation occurred in the central historic areas. Shelling, barrel bombs and the deadly tunnel bombs able to wipe out entire buildings in a single blow resulted in the massive and in many cases irreversible destruction of historical heritage sites. This includes the largest and oldest mosque in Aleppo, the Great Umayyad Mosque (Alafandi and Rahim 2014), a masterpiece of Islamic architecture, which suffered major damage during the conflict including the collapse of its eleventh-century minaret. Many centuries-old suqs and khans as well as many other buildings from different historical periods have been destroyed, either partially or completely. The world-famous Aleppo Citadel was also damaged, albeit to a lesser degree.

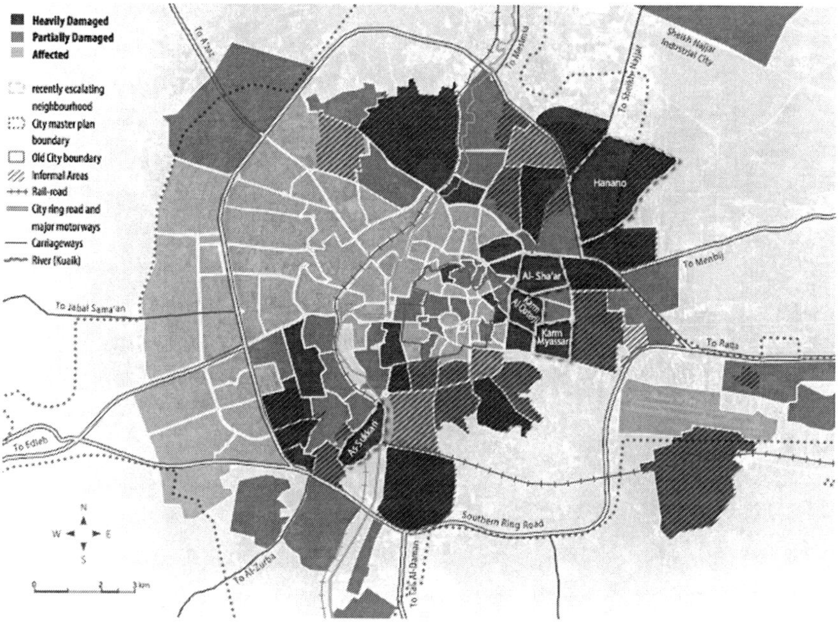

Figure 2.2: Damage assessment for the city of Aleppo.
Source: UN-Habitat (2014: 9).

The extent of the destruction of the physical assets alone is an indicator of the magnitude of the challenge ahead. According to a UNESCO-UNITAR report (2018),[5] at the end of 2016, over 33,500 structures within the urban area had been damaged, with the extent of the damage varying from a maximum of 65 per cent of structures in the neighbourhood of Al-Aqabeh, in the central part of the city, to 50 per cent in some of the peripheral neighbourhoods. Especially high levels of destruction occurred in the north-eastern neighbourhoods and in the south-eastern quadrant of the city (Figure 2.4).

The damage to the important heritage sites located in the central areas of the city (Figure 2.5) was thoroughly assessed in 2017 by the AKTC (2018a). This

5 For a comprehensive analysis of the damage to cities during the Syrian crisis, see REACH and UNITAR (2019). See also UN-Habitat (2014).

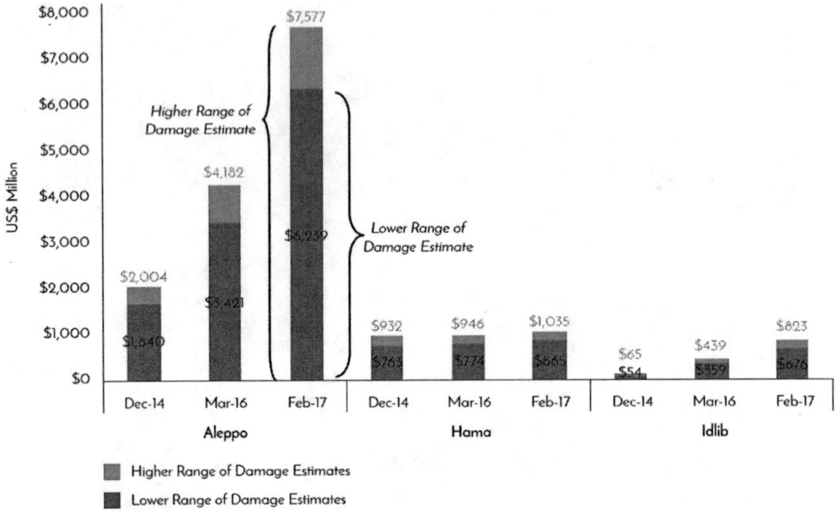

Figure 2.3: Estimate of the increase in damages to Aleppo's city infrastructure from 2014 to 2017 (million US dollars).

Source: World Bank (2017: iii).

assessment constitutes a fundamental tool for the reconstruction and recovery process of the Ancient City and focuses on three specific areas: (a) the Great Mosque and the historic suqs, (b) the Citadel and its surroundings, and (c) the nearby residential areas of Bab al-Ahmar and Al-Bayyada.[6]

Area of the Great Mosque and of the historic suqs. Over 40 per cent of the structures in this area were either lost or badly damaged, requiring either full or partial reconstruction. Significant damage was suffered by the most important monument in the area, the Great Umayyad Mosque.[7] The suqs and khans were

6 Besides these core zones, several other areas rich in historical monuments and cultural infrastructure in Aleppo suffered heavy damage during the war. An example is the Aleppo Museum, which was severely damaged by bombing in 2014. Fortunately, all the collections had been previously removed and sheltered by the DGAM. Another significant case is the Armenian Forty Martyrs Cathedral, destroyed in 2015.

7 The construction of the Great Mosque of Aleppo began in AD 715 AD under Umayyad Caliph Al-Walid and was completed in AD 717 by his successor Umayyad Caliph Suleyman. The minaret was built during the early Islamic period, around AD 1089. The mosque was included in UNESCO's World Heritage list in 1986.

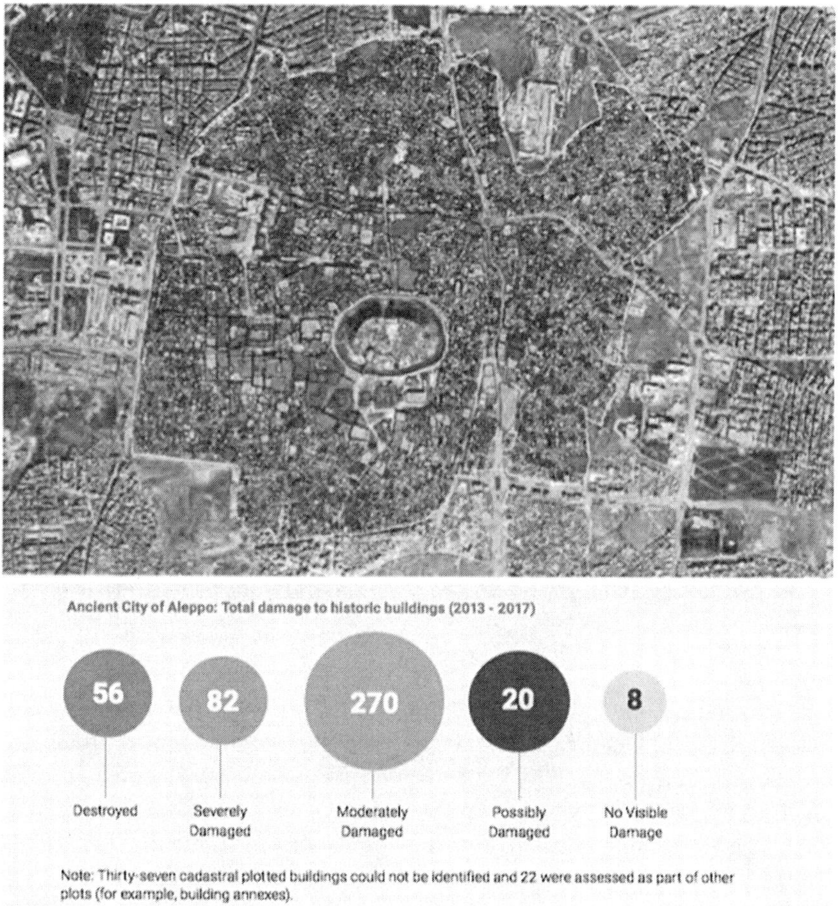

Figure 2.4: Old City of Aleppo: damage to historic buildings.
Source: UNESCO and UNITAR (2018: 29).

also severely affected: of the total surface of the suqs existing before the conflict, it is estimated that 82 per cent still exists, while approximately 15,000 square metres (sqm) of space were lost as a result of the recent conflict. However, most of the sections of the suqs have experienced damage and have been inoperative for many years. The remaining historic fabric (roughly 60 per cent) is partially damaged, requiring reconstruction or rehabilitation.

The Great Mosque. In this area, the most significant loss was the destruction of parts of the Great Umayyad Mosque since 2012 and the tearing down of its

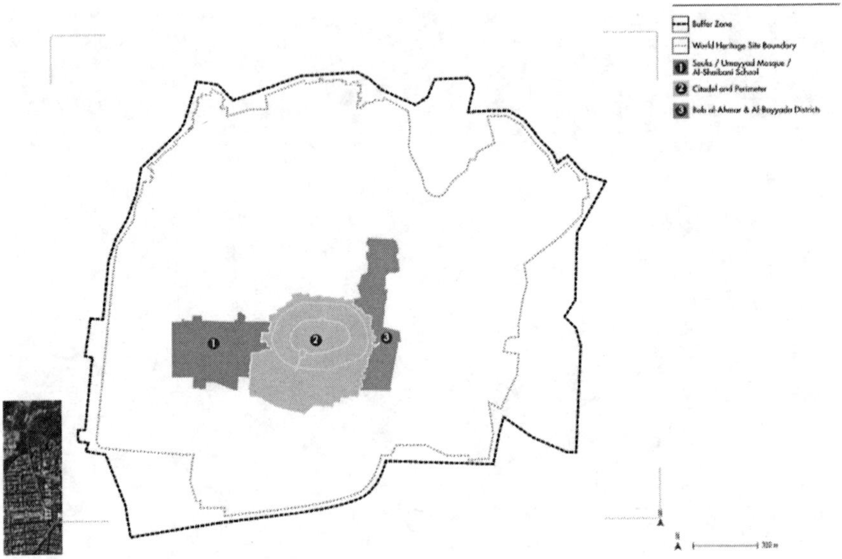

Figure 2.5: The three central areas where the damage assessment was carried out.
Source: AKTC (2018a).

eleventh-century minaret in 2013 (Figures 2.6, 2.7 and 2.8). The mosque was initially damaged in October 2012 during clashes between the armed groups and was subsequently occupied by the rebel forces. Heavy fighting continued in the area throughout 2016. Explosions produced cracks in the structure, while many precious historical manuscripts were looted. The historical wooden minbar was dismantled and looted, and many wooden doors were burned.

The historic Al-Mdineh suqs. With their long and narrow alleys, the al-Mdineh suqs constituted the largest covered historic market in the world,[8] with an

8 Al-Mdineh suqs are located between the Citadel and the Antakya Gate, at the heart of the Old City of Aleppo (listed as a World Heritage site since 1986). During the Seleucid and Roman periods, a colonnaded street led up to the Citadel hill from the west, where the south area of the Old City still retains the Hellenistic grid street plan. Little is known about the development of the suqs area during the Byzantine and Early Islamic periods. Some sections of the suqs could date back to the fourteenth and fifteenth centuries and were named after various professions and crafts, hence the wool suq, the copper suq and so on. At the end of the fifteenth century, most of the roofs of the suqs were made of wood. A vast campaign of construction of suqs and khans was begun during

Figure 2.6: Aerial photo of the Great Mosque after it was damaged.
Source: AKTC (2018a).

approximate length of 13 kilometres, and a surface area of around 16 hectares. The al-Mdineh suqs area contained around 6,000 shops and fifteen caravanserais. It was a major trading centre for imported luxury goods, such as raw silk from Iran, spices and dyes from India and many other imported products, as well as local products such as wool, agricultural products and soap.

Many sections of the suqs and other medieval buildings in the Ancient City were destroyed, ruined or burnt as a result of fighting that began on September 2012. Most of the suqs were severely damaged and several vaults were destroyed (Figures 2.9 and 2.10). The damage to the al-Mdineh suqs resulted not only in the disappearance of a unique piece of the remarkable historical and cultural

the Ottoman period, at the beginning of the sixteenth century. After two major fires, the Ottoman authorities covered the suqs with stone vaults and domes.

Figure 2.7: The destruction of the minaret of the Great Mosque, 24 April 2013.
Source: AKTC (2017c).

heritage of the Old City, but most importantly in the destruction of the commercial emblem of Aleppo, the economic capital of Syria.

The Citadel and its surroundings. During the conflict, the Citadel (Figure 2.11)[9] was the site of several clashes between governmental and opposition forces. Parts of the walls of the Citadel, a tower and some of the internal buildings suffered damage. In the interior of the Citadel the destruction was relatively contained, affecting only ten structures, whose combined surface area totals 10,300 sqm,

9 The Citadel of Aleppo, a medieval fortress considered to be one of the oldest in the world, had been occupied since the middle of the third millennium BCE. It bears the traces of many cultures and civilizations, including the Greeks, the Byzantines, the Ayyubids and the Mamluks. The Citadel was included in UNESCO's World Heritage list in 1986.

Figure 2.8: The Great Mosque of Aleppo: damage to the exterior and interior.
Source: Author's photos.

one-third of which was heavily damaged and the remaining parts moderately affected (Figure 2.12).

The walls and towers along the north and east sides, which were directly exposed to fire, suffered significant damage. More extensive losses resulting from the conflict were concentrated on the south-east side of the fortified Citadel and include, among other structures, the Madrasahs al-Sultaniyya and Khosrwiyya and the Mosque of al-Utrush. Two very important buildings dating from modern times, the New Serai and the Former National Hospital (Carlton Hotel), were completely destroyed by tunnel bombs (Figure 2.13).

The damage assessment indicates that over 52 per cent of the structures, or thirty-nine buildings, with a total surface area of 119,000 sqm, experienced either total collapse or heavy damage, mostly concentrated in the large structures located in the south-east sector outside of the Citadel. The remaining damage was either partial or limited and affected a total of sixty-six buildings, comprising a surface area of over 53,000 sqm. Forty-two of these buildings are residential structures of limited dimensions.

Figure 2.9: Historic Suqs area: general damage assessment.
Source: AKTC (2018a).

Figure 2.10: Aleppo, the historic Suqs, before and after.
Source: Yaghi (2017: 21).

Figure 2.11: Area of the Citadel: general damage assessment.
Source: AKTC (2018a).

The residential areas of Bab al-Ahmar and Al-Bayyada. In these two neighbourhoods (Figure 2.14) the damage is relatively less severe than in the case of the suqs and Citadel, amounting to a combined total of around 20 per cent of the total building stock. Partial damage is also limited (21 per cent), with most of the structures moderately or lightly affected (59.7 per cent). Out of a total of 588 damaged buildings, 572 are residential structures, totalling a surface area of approximately 87,000 sqm.

2.3 Responses during the crisis

During the conflict, national and international heritage conservation specialist organizations had very limited opportunities for intervention.[10] While some actions were taken to prevent damage, support for the administration in charge of local heritage protection was limited and very often possible only outside of

10 For a complete list of initiatives in support of Syria's cultural heritage, see Perini and Cunliffe (2014).

Figure 2.12: Aleppo, the Citadel: the main entrance gate and the Ottoman post.
Sources: Yaghi (2017: 19); DGAM (2015).

Figure 2.13: The destruction of the Carlton Hotel with a tunnel bomb in May 2014.
Source: Yaghi (2017: 12).

Figure 2.14: Residential districts area: general damage assessment and view.
Sources: AKTC (2018a) and Author's photo.

the country. The following are examples of activities that were carried out in the course of the conflict (DGAM 2019a):

- The DGAM undertook important efforts to preserve cultural heritage, rescue works of art and relocate objects from museums to safe havens.
- UNESCO, in collaboration with the International Council on Monuments and Sites (ICOMOS) and the International Centre for the Study of the Preservation and Restoration of Cultural Property (ICCROM), from 2014 implemented an EU-funded programme,[11] supported also by Flanders and Austria, aimed at supporting technical meetings and technical training activities, conducted in Beirut, Italy and, after 2016, Aleppo.
- ICCROM, through its Sharjah office, was able to organize a short course series on the conservation and documentation of built cultural heritage, as well as international fora to raise awareness of the situation of Aleppo and the Syrian sites.
- ICOMOS, in co-operation with the US-based Foundation Cyark, through Project Anqa (Akhtar et al. 2017), funded by the UK-based Arcadia Fund, contributed to the 3D recording of six at-risk heritage sites in Syria and capacity-building for Syrian professionals, with the aim of fostering the creation of a sustainable 3D architectural inventory.
- The US-based foundation Global Heritage Fund (GHF) launched the project AMAL (mobile and web application for rapid damage assessment of cultural heritage sites in conflict zones) in partnership with ICOMOS, ICCROM, the Bahrein-based Arab Regional Centre for World Heritage (ARC-WH) and the Dutch Prince Claus Fund, which has also provided training to Syrian professionals.

---

11 The Emergency Safeguarding of the Syrian Heritage Project was launched on 1 March 2014 for a period of three years. The overall objective of the project was to contribute to restoring social cohesion, stability and sustainable development through the protection and safeguarding of cultural heritage. The project adopted a three-pronged approach: (a) monitor and assess the cultural heritage situation in Syria through updated and continued knowledge and documentation through the establishment of an International Observatory of Syrian Cultural Heritage; (b) mitigate the destruction and loss of Syrian cultural heritage through national and international awareness-raising efforts; and (c) protect and safeguard Syrian cultural heritage through enhanced technical assistance and capacity-building for national stakeholders and beneficiaries. The project was subsequently extended for a year and terminated in 2018.

- The US-based foundation World Monuments Fund (WMF) organized technical training programmes in Jordan for Syrian and Jordanian professionals to build the capacities needed for heritage reconstruction.
- The German Archaeological Institute (DAI), within the framework of the project funded by Germany on 'Capacity Building, Technical and Media Support for the Protection of Syrian Cultural Heritage', organized workshops in Beirut and Berlin to enhance Syrian professionals' capacities in recording, storing and analysing cultural heritage research data.

2.4 Emergency post-war initiatives for Aleppo

At the end of the conflict in late 2016, some urgent initiatives for the stabilization and safeguarding of the damaged monuments in view of future restoration activities were launched. The most significant initiatives implemented so far have included the following:

Removal of debris. The removal of debris (Figure 2.15) from destroyed or damaged buildings has been conducted in various parts of the city by different actors, including the Governorate of Aleppo, private non-governmental organizations (NGOs) (in particular the Syrian Trust for Development) and individual citizens. The United Nations Development Programme (UNDP) has provided major financial and operational support to this operation.[12] For the historic areas, the removal of debris has been carried out under the supervision of the DGAM, with the support of UNESCO and UNDP and of the Governorate of Aleppo.[13] The removal needs to be closely controlled, as the debris can contain relevant architectural or archaeological elements that have value for the restoration of the major buildings. At the present time, over 70 per cent of the affected areas have been cleared.

---

12 See UNDP website: *Solid Waste and Debris Management Project*, https://open.undp.org/projects/00113684.

13 'The Governorate carried out documentation and sorting of archaeological debris and rubble removal to open the road axes and roads of the ancient city in many areas including: the area surrounding the Umayyad Mosque, Khan al-Wazir, Bab al-Hadid, Bab Antakya, Bab al-Nairab, Bab al-Maqam, Suq al-Qutton, Suq al-Zahrawi, Suq al-Zourb, Suq al-Attaren, Suq al-Haddadin, the vicinity of al-Sayaf mosque, al-Jadida area, the perimeter of al-Abraj mosque, Khan al-Albayeh, Suq al-Gokh, Suq al Zahr, al Nahaseen Suq, al Jubailian area, al-Bandara area' (DGAM 2019b: 5).

Figure 2.15: Removal of debris in the Aleppo old Suq.

Sources: AP/Ammar (2018); DGAM (2019b: 6).

Consolidation of damaged buildings. The restoration of the majority of the destroyed building and structures will require studies, design work and careful rebuilding processes that will take time. It was therefore urgent to consolidate some of the damaged structures to avoid further collapse and to prepare for future work.
Protection of the ruins. The ruins of damaged buildings and structures have been protected and fenced off to avoid the removal of materials and of decorative parts.

2.5 Restoration initiatives

While very little could be done to prevent the massive destruction of cultural heritage sites during the conflict, several initiatives were taken to document the situation and prepare for future reconstruction (WHC 2015; Grandin 2015; Saad and Stellmach 2015). As soon as reconstruction activity was possible, in November 2016, a number of planning meetings were organized by the Beirut UNESCO office (UNESCO 2017a, 2017b, 2017c). This effort resulted in the preparation of a comprehensive planning document that served as a guideline for the initial phases of intervention. Unfortunately, UNESCO did not support this co-ordination effort after the end of the EU-financed project in 2018. Other UN organizations, however, have remained active in the city, and have contributed substantially to the first phase of the reconstruction effort. This includes UNDP, which took care of the debris removal and the rehabilitation of parts of the market areas, mostly outside the historic core, as well as other UN organizations active in humanitarian assistance. Recently, six UN agencies (Food and Agriculture Organization, UNDP, UN Population Fund, UN-Habitat, UNICEF and World Food Programme) joined hands and proposed a Joint Programme to Strengthen Urban and Rural Resilience and the Conditions for Recovery in Syria,[14] which, while not specifically focused on historic heritage, can provide useful support to the overall recovery process. This programme, which will certainly address the situation of the historic areas of Aleppo, aims to promote

14 The project, yet to be officially validated at the time of this writing, will be supported initially by the European Union with a grant of 19 million US dollars over two years. Under UN Security Council Resolution 2254, during the 'Supporting Syria and the Region' conference in 2016, the UN committed to start to plan 'to coordinate civilian stabilization, post-conflict peacebuilding and recovery efforts' to be ready immediately after an agreement, in accordance with the framework for political transition put down in the Geneva Communique of 2012. That has resulted in the Post-Agreement Planning Process, under which 'Social Cohesion, Reconciliation and Peacebuilding' is a priority area.

area-based recovery and neighbourhood plans responsive to community needs, with particular emphasis on the most vulnerable groups. It will address the rehabilitation of basic services, to improve social resilience and cohesion and foster economic recovery and social inclusion.

Civil society organizations and academic institutions are also contributing to shaping a vision for the recovery and reconstruction of Aleppo. In particular, the conservation community has discussed the issue of reconstruction of the destroyed monuments from the point of view of the preservation of their authenticity (Labadidi 2017; Lafi 2017; Munawar 2018). Others have analysed the process of urban reconstruction in a broader context, considering the great social transformations that the city witnessed in the years of the conflict (Qudsi 2016; Sandes 2017; Swaid et al. 2016; Dayoub 2015).

The DGAM has taken a leading role in defining the policy directions for the recovery and reconstruction process, by drafting initial planning documents (DGAM 2018) and defining the 'Vision' for the process (DGAM 2019a). In terms of international policy-making, the World Heritage Committee has played a role in monitoring the situation since the beginning of the conflict; inscribing all the World Heritage sites in Syria, including the Old City of Aleppo, in the World Heritage in Danger list; and issuing recommendations for the recovery process. While these recommendations have not been supported by concrete actions on the ground, they nevertheless constitute guidance for future interventions.[15]

The limited local resources available for the reconstruction and the current lack of international support constitute the major obstacles to a rapid recovery of the Old City of Aleppo. In order to promote a concrete approach to reconstruction and to facilitate fund-raising, AKTC has produced a list of twenty-five urgent projects that could be financed by donors (AKTC 2018c). The main initiatives that were launched after the stabilization of the situation in the City of Aleppo are the following:

The Great Mosque. Following an initial assessment by the AKTC (2017b), the local technical (DGAM) and religious (Waqf) authorities have co-ordinated some protective work, mostly focused on preserving and ordering the stones of the minaret in preparation for its reconstruction and on replacing some of the damaged sections of the mosque (Figure 2.16). The restoration work, financed by the Republic of Chechnya in the amount of 1.4 million US dollars, and prepared by the Civil Engineering and Architecture Faculty of Aleppo University,

15 See in particular Decision 43 COM 7A.31, adopted during the 43rd session of the World Heritage Committee in Baku in July 2019 (WHC 2019).

Figure 2.16: The Great Mosque (the stones of the minaret are currently being reordered in the courtyard of the mosque; some initial restoration work is visible in the background).

Source: Author's photos.

was begun in late 2018. The interior of the mosque has been consolidated, as some of the pillars had suffered damage (Figure 2.17). A laboratory was set up to construct new wooden doors and ornaments for the mosque. The initial resources were allocated for the reconstruction of the minaret. However, this task will require extensive preparation for the engineering and architectural design work and for the procurement of the means and materials needed to rebuild the monument. Although its structure had been studied in the past (Fangi and Wahbeh 2013), this complex task requires sophisticated technical skills that are available internationally, but that cannot at the moment be fully mobilized due to the sanctions regime.

The historical Al-Mdineh suqs. In the area of the suqs (AKTC 2017a), a model restoration project has been implemented by the AKTC in the Suq al-Saqatiyya (Figure 2.18). The suq contains twenty-six shops in its eastern section and fifty-four shops in its northern section. The project has involved the complete restoration of the damaged domes and structures, the construction of a new and modern technical installation (water, electricity, air conditioning, etc.) and the design of appropriate functional and decorative elements (portals for the shops, lighting, etc.) in harmony with the historic character of the site (Figure 2.19). The restoration of this suq aims to experiment with innovative technical solutions for

Figure 2.17: Damaged pillars in the interior of the Great Mosque (dismantling and reconstruction).
Source: Author's photos.

the reconstruction of the ancient market of Aleppo. This project, completed in July 2019, is intended to pave the way for a larger reconstruction process of the historical al-Mdineh suqs (AKTC 2018d).

The Citadel. Restoration of some parts of the Citadel has already been carried out. In particular, in 2017, the restoration work on the staircase at the entrance of the Citadel was initiated by the DGAM in co-ordination with UNESCO and AKTC. In order to co-ordinate the restoration process, a workshop was organized for governmental staff (DGAM, Governorate, Directorate of the Old City, University, Waqf) as well as independent contributors (students, private-sector architects and engineers), for a total of around sixty persons. Furthermore, a training workshop for local artisans and technicians in stone work and stone masonry techniques was organized by the DGAM and AKTC with the support of UNESCO (AKTC 2017d). This programme facilitated the speedy restoration of some of the damaged structures inside the Citadel, namely the Mill Tower and the Barracks of Ibrahim Pasha, which used to host the visitor centre of the Citadel (Figure 2.20). The archaeological areas of the Citadel suffered reparable

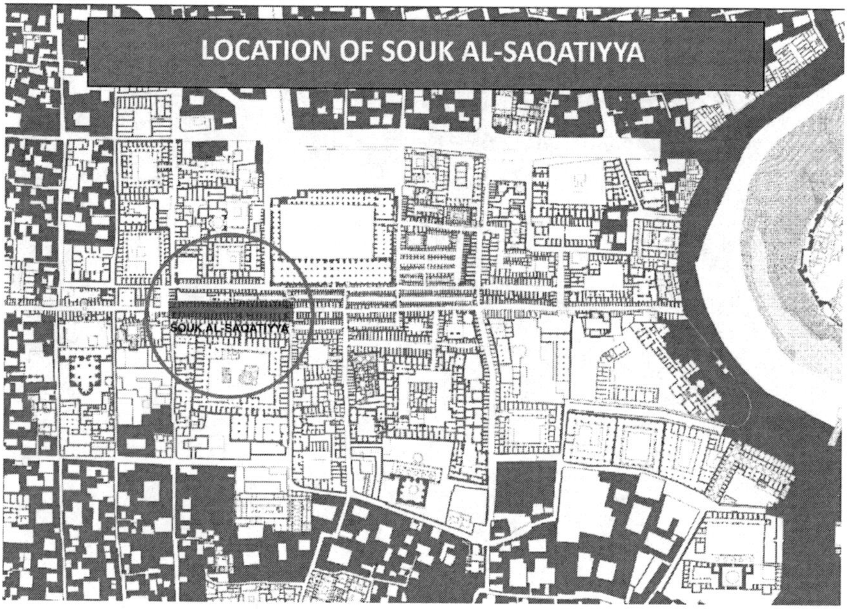

Figure 2.18: Location of the Suq al-Saqatiyya.
Source: AKTC (2018d).

Figure 2.19: The Suq al-Saqatiyya before and after the restoration.
Source: AKTC (2018d).

Figure 2.20: Citadel: Mill Tower after restoration.
Source: Author's photo.

damage during the conflict, and most of the internal structures have already been restored.

Other initiatives. In co-operation with UNDP, the Aleppo Chamber of Commerce, the Union of Craftsmen and the Aleppo City Council, five suqs (199 shops) were rehabilitated and reopened in June 2019 in the Ancient City (al-Nahasin, al-Khabya, al-Mahmas, al-Sham, al-Zahrawi). Restoration work is ongoing in other suqs, such as al-Attarin and al-Zarb. The Aleppo Governorate is pursuing efforts to rehabilitate several schools in the Ancient City, while the Ministry of Awqaf is restoring some religious buildings with the support of local and international donors. Conservation and restoration works are being carried out at Bab al-Faraj Clock Tower, on the initiative of local NGOs, including some archaeological excavations around the site, while the documentation and structural analysis of Beit Ghazaleh and Beit Ajiqbash (Museum of Folk Arts) were carried out with the support of a team of specialists in 3D scanning technologies. Other restoration works that are under way or have been completed include the famous thirteenth-century Hammam Bab al-Ahmar, partially damaged during the war, which was restored and reopened in 2017; the Bashita Mosque, built in 1350, in the Al-Aqaba district; and the small Al-Akhal Mosque, built in 1485. The restoration of Beit Bassel, Hammam Bab al-Ahmar were completed in addition to many private houses and shops. Initial restoration studies were done for many buildings such as Al-Hatab Square, Bab Qinnasrin, Beit Ala'a Tower and the western tower of Bab Antakiya, but these have not yet been implemented for lack of funds. The rehabilitation of religious buildings is also currently being planned, including the Forty Martyrs Cathedral of the Armenians, located on the north-west side of Aleppo Castle in the Saliba neighbourhood; the Cathedral of Our Lady of the Roman Catholics; and the Cathedral of Mar Elias of the Maronites in El Jadida.[16]

2.6 A new governance framework for the reconstruction and recovery process

Before the crisis, the management of the Old City was the responsibility of the local governments (Municipality and Governorate) of Aleppo, and was directly implemented by a Directorate for the Old City. The Committee for the Protection of the Ancient City, which included representatives of the professions and civil society, was also established after the inscription of the Old City in UNESCO's World Heritage list in 1986.[17] However, the complexity of the current situation has prompted a reflection on the need to create a new governance framework able to effectively co-ordinate activities in full respect of the conservation principles enshrined in the World Heritage status of the city, and to prepare and implement a Reconstruction and Recovery Master Plan.

A document recently submitted to UNESCO by the Syrian Government (DGAM 2019a) foresees the creation of two new technical bodies that could be charged with the task of co-ordinating the reconstruction and recovery process: (a) the Committee for the Reconstruction and Recovery of the Ancient City, and (b) the Agency for the Reconstruction and Recovery of the Ancient City.

---

16 Source: communication of DGAM, 29 August 2019.

17 The Ancient City of Aleppo was inscribed in the World Heritage list in 1986, based on two of the criteria foreseen in the Operational Guidelines (Criteria III and IV), reflecting, respectively, the exceptional importance of its cultural traditions and of its past and living civilizations, and the outstanding quality of the architectural outcomes of the different stages of its history.

The Committee for the Reconstruction and Recovery of the Ancient City of Aleppo. Based on the experience of past decades, the new committee will have a mandate to co-ordinate all future interventions in the historic urban area as well as to generate consensus among the different stakeholders on priorities and important decisions. This committee will include the key actors in the reconstruction and recovery process, that is, the national and local authorities, namely the Ministry of Culture for the intervention on the heritage assets, the Ministry of Waqf for the religious buildings, the Ministry of Local Government for the local administrative processes, the Aleppo Governorate, the Municipality of Aleppo for the management of the interventions on site, as well as other significant national and international partners.

The Agency for the Reconstruction and Recovery of the Ancient City of Aleppo. This specialized agency will co-ordinate and execute all studies and plans for the restoration of historical monuments and the rehabilitation of buildings, the restoration and maintenance of public spaces, and the social and economic revitalization of the Ancient City. The proposed agency's structure is based on a collaborative framework involving the existing technical structures active in the Ancient City, both at national and local level. Co-operation with national and international NGOs is also considered a key condition to acquire the needed technical and financial assistance.[18] This extends also to the international development and humanitarian assistance organizations active in the country, such as UNDP, UNESCO, UNICEF and others.

The Reconstruction and Recovery Master Plan. In order to guide and co-ordinate the activities for the physical reconstruction and restoration of the Ancient City of Aleppo, the Vision document foresees the preparation of a Reconstruction and Recovery Master Plan, focused primarily on the perimeter of the World Heritage site.[19] The plan will give priority to projects able to provide solutions for addressing social and economic needs and for speeding up the recovery process. It is intended to be based on extensive public consultations to involve citizens and stakeholders in the process.

The Master Plan will address the following aspects of the reconstruction and recovery process: (a) civic participation; (b) identification of priorities and

18 The Vision document mentions in particular the Syria Trust for Development and the Aga Khan Cultural Services, the local organization of the Aga Khan Development Network (AKDN).

19 A specific Management Plan for the World Heritage site, according to the Guidelines of the World Heritage Convention, is also foreseen for a later phase of the planning process.

medium- and long-term initiatives; (c) management of regulatory and approval processes; (d) management of zoning and building laws; (e) design and improvement of infrastructural networks (roads, utilities, sewage, etc.); and (f) preparation of Special Area Plans.

Some key constraints to the implementation of these governance and planning innovations have been clearly identified in the document. The issue of true ownership or established tenancy rights of the current occupiers of a building would need to be established ahead of any rehabilitation efforts. Many of the residents and shopkeepers who fled at the height of the crisis are now coming back to Aleppo. Such spontaneous development is likely to continue and needs to be managed to avoid impediments to the smooth implementation of the initiatives.

The most critical issue currently is the lack of adequate financial support for the reconstruction and recovery process. The sanctions imposed by the western powers have targeted primarily the system of financial transactions of the country, making it almost impossible to launch a comprehensive reconstruction effort. While humanitarian assistance has been in part exempted from the sanctions, all activities falling under the category 'development', including urban reconstruction, have suffered restrictions. In spite of this situation, some resource mobilization has been possible through national NGOs, ministries and local governments.

With international aid hampered by the sanctions, some limited interventions in support of recovery and reconstruction have been promoted by UNDP and by the AKTC. In addition, microfinance institutions supported by the Syria Trust for Development and by the Aga Khan Microfinancing are already active in Aleppo and are rapidly extending their range of activities, with positive impacts on the livelihood of individuals and on the prospects of businesses hit by the crisis. The local private sector has also supported reconstruction of private property, and while most of the work remains to be done, some signs of recovery are evident in many parts of the Old City (the reopening of shops, restaurants, hotels, etc.). Finally, some international foundations have expressed interest in supporting technical assistance activities, special area projects, training and capacity-building as soon as the political situation allows.

Conclusions

In the wake of one of the most destructive conflicts in its millenary history, Aleppo is trying to revitalize itself (Abdulkarim 2016). While the highest priority has to be given to humanitarian assistance for the impoverished population and displaced persons, the international, national and local institutions involved have reaffirmed the importance of putting culture and heritage up front in the reconstruction and recovery process. This reflects an approach developed internationally in recent decades, following the increasing destruction of cultural heritage sites in recent conflicts (UNESCO and World Bank 2018) and is also a response to the expectations of the affected populations, who see in the rehabilitation of historical heritage a fundamental symbol of hope and regeneration.

The reconstruction and recovery of the Old City of Aleppo is a huge task that will require many decades of collective and individual effort. Unfortunately, the current political stalemate is limiting the opportunities and the pace of recovery of this extraordinary historic city. In spite of the current outlook, however, several initiatives have been carried out, stressing the importance of heritage preservation in the reconstruction process as a tool to stimulate local initiative through financial and regulatory policies, reactivate the economic systems that were at the core of Aleppo's life throughout many centuries, and provide the local population with opportunities for work and social integration.

References

Abdulkarim, Maamoun (2016), 'Challenges Facing Cultural Institutions in Times of Conflict: Syrian Cultural Heritage', in *Post-Trauma Reconstruction. Vol. 2: Colloquium Proceedings Appendices*, Charenton-le-Pont, ICOMOS International Secretariat, p. 9–10, http://openarchive.icomos.org/1707

Akhtar, Saima et al. (2017), 'Project Anqa: Digitizing and Documenting Cultural Heritage in the Middle East', in *The International Archives of the Photogrammetry, Remote Sensing and Spatial Information Sciences*, Vol. XLII-2/W5, p. 1–5, https://doi.org/10.5194/isprs-archives-XLII-2-W5-1-2017

AKTC-Aga Khan Trust for Culture (2017a), *Aleppo: Reconstruction and Rehabilitation of the Suqs*. Project Brief, Geneva, AKTC, October

AKTC (2017b), *Old City of Aleppo. Action Area Plan, Phase 1*, Geneva, AKTC, May

AKTC (2017c), *Reconstruction of the Umayyad Mosque Minaret, Aleppo*. Technical Report, Project Guidelines and Methodology, Geneva, AKTC, September

AKTC (2017d), *Vocational Training in Stone Masonry and Restoration Techniques*. Technical Report, Geneva, AKTC, December

AKTC (2018a), *Old City of Aleppo. Building Information and Preliminary Damage Assessment in Three Pilot Conservation Areas*, Geneva, AKTC

AKTC (2018b), *Plan of Rehabilitation and Economic Rehabilitation Process of the Historic Souks of Aleppo. Potential Extensions. Phase One*, Geneva, AKTC

AKTC (2018c), *Potential Rehabilitation Projects: Old City of Aleppo*. Project brief, Aleppo, AKTC

AKTC (2018d), *Rehabilitation of the Saqatiyya Suq*. Technical Report, Geneva, AKTC, May

AKTC (2019), *Ancient City of Aleppo Action Area Plan*, Geneva, AKTC

Alafandi, Rami and Asiah Abdul Rahim (2014), 'Umayyad Mosque in Aleppo. Yesterday, Today and Tomorrow', in *International Journal of Arts & Sciences*, Vol. 7, No. 5, p. 319–347, http://www.universitypublications.net/ijas/0705/html/H4V574.xml

Ammar, Hassan (2018), 'In Syria's Aleppo, Old Bazaar Struggles to Come Back Tto Life', in *AP Images*, 22 January, https://apimagesblog.com/blog/2018/1/22/in-syrias-aleppo-old-bazaar-struggles-to-come-back-to-life

Awford, Jenny (2014), 'Satellite Images Show Devastation Caused to 290 Cultural Sites by Syrian Conflict . . .', in *MailOnline*, 23 December, http://dailym.ai/1t7D8k4

Bevan, Robert (2006), *The Destruction of Memory. Architecture at War*, London, Reaktion Books

Bianca, Stefano (2000), *Urban Form in the Arab World. Past and Present*, London, Thames & Hudson

Bianca, Stefano (2007), *Syria. Medieval Citadels Between East and West*, Torino, Allemandi for the Aga Khan Trust for Culture,https://archnet.org/publications/5189

Bianca, Stefano et al. (1980), *The Conservation of the Old City of Aleppo*, Paris, UNESCO, https://unesdoc.unesco.org/ark:/48223/pf0000042161

Burns, Ross (2017), *Aleppo: A History*, London/New York, Routledge

Busquets, Joan, ed. (2005), *Aleppo. Rehabilitation of the Old City*, Cambridge/London, Harvard Graduate School of Design

David, Jean-Claude and Gérard Degeorge (2002), *Alep*, Paris, Flammarion

Dayoub, Dima (2015), *Wartime Coping and Its Re-configuration of the Urban Space. The Case of Aleppo City During the Protracted Syrian Conflict*, M.A. Thesis, University of Stuttgart

DGAM-Syrian Ministry of Culture Directorate-General of Antiquities and Museums (2015), *Ancient City of Aleppo: New Photos of Current Statue at the Citadel*, 1 June, http://www.dgam.gov.sy/?d=314&id=1717

DGAM (2018), *The Intervention Plan for Aleppo Ancient City*, Damascus, DGAM

DGAM (2019a), *The Reconstruction and Recovery of the Ancient City of Aleppo. Vision and Planning Framework*, Damascus, DGAM

DGAM (2019b), *State Party Report on the State of Conservation of the Syrian Cultural Heritage Sites (Ancient City of Aleppo)*, Report submitted to the 43rd session of the World Heritage Committee held in Baku on 30 June-10 July, https://whc.unesco.org/document/171576

DOC-Directorate of the Old City and GTZ (1998), *Project for the Rehabilitation of the Old City of Aleppo. Development Plan for the Old City of Aleppo*, Aleppo, DOC

DOC and GTZ (2005), *Old City of Aleppo. Conservation and Development Strategy*, Aleppo, DOC

Fangi, Gabriele and Wissam Wahbeh (2013), 'The Destroyed Minaret of the Umayyad Mosque of Aleppo. The Survey of the Original State', in *European Scientific Journal Special Edition*, Vol. 4 (December), p. 403–409, https://eujournal.org/index.php/esj/article/view/2492

Glass, Charles (2016), *Syria Burning: A Short History of a Catastrophe*, London/New York, Verso

Gokalp, Esref and Fuat Uguz (2018), *The Reconstruction of Aleppo's Historic Center*, Thesis, Politecnico di Milano, http://hdl.handle.net/10589/143681

Grandin, Thierry (2015), *Proposed Materials and Considerations for the Reconstruction of the Ancient City of Aleppo*. Draft Proposal, Paris, UNESCO

Jodido, Philip, ed. (2011), *The Aga Khan Historic Cities Programme. Strategies for Urban Regeneration*, Munich/London/New York, Prestel, p. 244–247, https://archnet.org/publications/6725

Lababidi, Rim (2017), 'The Old City of Aleppo. Situation Analysis', in *e-dialogos*, No. 6 (June), p. 9–19, http://www.diadrasis.org/public/files/edialogos_006-LABABIDI.pdf

Lafi, Nora (2017), 'Building and Destroying Authenticity in Aleppo: Heritage between Conservation, Transformation, Destruction, and Re-invention', in Christoph Bernhardt, Martin Sabrow, Achim Saupe, eds, *Gebaute Geschichte. Historische Authentizität im Stadtraum*, Göttingen, Wallstein, p. 206–228, https://hal.archives-ouvertes.fr/halshs-01560321

Munawar, Nour A. (2018), 'Rebuilding Aleppo: Public Engagement in Post-Conflict Reconstruction', in *ICOMOS University Forum*, No. 1, http://openarchive.icomos.org/1848

Neglia, Giulia Annalinda (2007), 'An Interpretation of the Urban Fabric: The Structure of Pre-Islamic Aleppo', in *Urban Morphology*, Vol. 11, No. 1 (April), p. 43–58, http://www.urbanform.org/online_unlimited/pdf2007/2007111_43-58.pdf

Perini, Silvia and Emma Cunliffe (2014), *Towards a Protection of the Syrian Cultural Heritage: A Summary of the International Responses (March 2011-March 2014)*, Girona, Heritage for Peace, https://eprint.ncl.ac.uk/244788

Qudsi, Jwanah (2016), *Rebuilding Old Aleppo. Postwar Sustainable Recovery and Urban Refugee Resettlement*, Essay submitted for the Master programme in International Urban Development Planning, New York University, https://icsd.wpengine.com/wp-content/uploads/2017/01/Qudsi.pdf

Ramadan, Mahmoud (2010), *Madinatuna – A Programme for Aleppo City Development Strategy 2025: Participation and the Role of Syrian Civil Society in the Local Urban Development*, Amsterdam, Hivos and Amsterdam University

Ramadan, Mahmoud (2012), *The Syrian City under the National Agenda for the Future of Syria*, Beirut, ESCWA-Economic and Social Commission for Western Asia

REACH Initiative and UNITAR-United Nations Institute for Training and Research (2019), *Syrian Cities Damage Atlas. Eight Year Anniversary of the Syrian Civil War: Thematic Assessment of Satellite Identified Damage*, 16 March, https://reliefweb.int/node/3038373

Saad, Ali and Thomas Stellmach (2010), *Aleppo Diverse | Open City. An Urban Vision for the Year 2025*, Berlin, UBERBAU/Syrian-German Technical Cooperation GTZ, https://www.bureaualisaad.eu/Aleppo-City-Vision

Saad, Ali and Thomas Stellmach (2015), 'Aleppo 2025 City Development Strategy: A Critical Reflection', in Robert Saliba, ed., *Urban Design in the Arab World. Reconceptualizing Boundaries*, London/New York, Routledge, p. 115–130

Sandes, Caroline A. (2017), 'Remembering Beirut: Lessons for Archaeology and (Post-) Conflict Urban Redevelopment in Aleppo', in *Ex Novo Journal of Archaeology*, Vol. 2 (December), p. 5–32, http://archaeologiaexnovo.org/2016/wp-content/uploads/2017/12/2_Sandes_ExNovo_2rev.pdf

Sauvaget, Jean (1941), *Alep. Essai sur le développement d'une grande ville syrienne, des origines au milieu du XIXème siècle*, Paris, Geuthner

Stürzbecher, Kurt, Jens Windelberg and Omar Abdul Aziz Hallaj (1998), *Development Plan of the Old City of Aleppo*, Aleppo, The Rehabilitation Project of the City of Aleppo

Swaid, Bashar et al. (2016), *Urban Gentrification and Challenges of Rehabilitation of the Historical Centre of Aleppo in the Post-War: Towards a Balanced Socio-economic Role*, paper presented at the 17th International Planning History Society Conference, Delft, July

Terao, Makoto (1995), 'Traditional Structure of the Old City, Aleppo: The Multiple Composition and the Vertical Articulation of the Urban Community in Aleppo', in *Keio Economic Studies*, Vol. 32, No. 1, p. 77–104, http://koara.lib.keio.ac.jp/xoonips/modules/xoonips/download.php/AA00260492-19950001-0077.pdf?file_id=28651

UN-Habitat (2014), *City Profile – Aleppo. Multi Sector Assessment*, Damascus, UN-Habitat, May, https://unhabitat.org/node/142348

UN-Habitat (2016), *Country Profile – Syria*, Damascus, UN-Habitat Syria Office, https://unhabitat.org/country-profile-syria

UNESCO (2017a), *UNESCO Hosts First International Coordination Meeting for the Recovery of Aleppo's Heritage*, 9 March, https://whc.unesco.org/en/news/1639

UNESCO (2017b), *Workshop on the Ancient City of Aleppo 'Aleppo, a responsibility and a challenge'*, Aleppo, Chahbaa Hotel, 15–16 March

UNESCO (2017c), *Experts Meet in Aleppo to Discuss Traditional Building Materials and Techniques*, 4 October, http://www.unesco.org/new/en/media-services/single-view/news/experts_meet_in_aleppo_to_discuss_traditional_building_mate/back/9597

UNESCO (2019), *State of Conservation of the Ancient City of Aleppo*, Report presented to the 43rd World Heritage Committee Session, Baku, Azerbaijan, https://whc.unesco.org/document/174156

UNESCO and UNITAR (2018), *Five Years of Conflict. The State of Cultural Heritage in the Ancient City of Aleppo. A Comprehensive Multi-temporal Satellite Imagery-based Damage Analysis for the Ancient City of Aleppo*, Paris, UNESCO / Geneva, UNITAR, https://unesdoc.unesco.org/ark:/48223/pf0000265826

UNESCO and World Bank (2018), *Culture in City Reconstruction and Recovery*, Paris/Washington, UNESCO/World Bank, https://unesdoc.unesco.org/ark:/48223/pf0000265981

Vale, Lawrence J. and Thomas J. Campanella, eds (2005), *The Resilient City: How Modern Cities Recover from Disaster*, Oxford, Oxford University Press

WHC-World Heritage Centre (2015), *Post-Conflict Reconstruction in the Middle East Context, and in the Old City of Aleppo in Particular. Concept Note* (Background document by Nada Al Hassan), Paris, 18–19 June, https://whc.unesco.org/en/events/1286

WHC (2019), *Decision 43 COM 7A.31: Ancient City of Aleppo (Syrian Arab Republic) (C 21)*, 43rd session of the World Heritage Committee, https://whc.unesco.org/en/decisions/7525

World Bank (2017), *Syria Damage Assessment of Selected Cities: Aleppo, Hama, Idlib. Phase III*, Washington, World Bank, March, http://documents.worldbank.org/curated/en/530541512657033401

Yaghi, Ayman (2017), *Restoration Protocol in Conflict Zones. Practical Insights from the Old City of Aleppo*, Cologne Institute of Conservation Science, https://www.academia.edu/36666862

Stefano de Martino

Chapter 3: The Italian Response to the Cultural Heritage Emergency in Iraq

3.1 Iraq and its archaeological heritage

The territory that now corresponds to the modern state of Iraq was once the homeland of the most important ancient Near Eastern civilizations. This is where the ruins of many famous cities, such as Uruk, Ur, Babylon, Assur, Nimrud, Nineveh and many others, are found.

The first discoveries of the Mesopotamian cultures date back to the middle of the nineteenth century, when Paul Émile Botta, the French consul at Mosul at that time, and his English colleague Austin Henry Layard, the British ambassador in Istanbul, started digging in northern Mesopotamia. As is well known, the magnificent sculptures and reliefs found at Nimrud and Nineveh by these two archaeologists were sent, respectively, to the Louvre and to the British Museum.

The Ottoman Empire showed no interest in pre-Islamic antiquities until Osman Hamdi Bey became the director of the Imperial Museum in Constantinople and drafted the first law on the protection of cultural heritage within the Empire, promulgated in 1884. From that time onwards, antiquities were no longer exported without the permission of the Imperial Museum.

We are unable to say how much interest and knowledge the local people had of Mesopotamian antiquities at that time. Gertrude Bell reported that boys living near Nimrud used to deface the Neo-Assyrian reliefs (Rothfield 2009: 6); however, it is known that families living in villages around Nineveh took their children there, and showed them the ruins of the ancient cities for educational purposes (Al-Aswad 2017).

After the First World War, the State of Iraq was set up under the British Mandate (Dodge 2003), and the British authorities were very much aware of the historical importance of the region under their rule. The former collaboration with archaeologists such as Leonard Woolley, Thomas Edward Lawrence and Bell had been of great importance during the collapse of the Ottoman Empire; hence, their influence in developing new political entities should not be ignored. Indeed, from the beginning the British occupying forces maintained the most important archaeological sites, and the ancient Mesopotamian heritage was perceived as a cohesive element for a new country that was inhabited by people of different religions and cultures, including Sunnis, Shiites and Kurds.

The British narrative on the foundation of the Iraqi state always stressed that this was an artificial creation, with the drawing of its borders attributed also to Bell (Rothfield 2009: 10). In reality, however, Iraq was not entirely a British invention (Kamel 2019: 189). To be more precise, it covered the area of the three former Ottoman administrative divisions (in Turkish *vilayets*) of Mosul, Baghdad and Basra, which were under the leadership of Baghdad (Nuri 2018).

According to the British view, Iraq was a new and modern *nation*, in need of a 'National Museum'. Hence the Iraq National Museum was founded in 1926 by Bell; in accordance with the British concept of Iraqi heritage, only pre-Islamic works of art were collected and exhibited there. Bell also wrote the first Iraqi Law of Antiquities (1924), which granted to foreign archaeologists the right to divide up the finds. This had previously been prohibited under the aforementioned Ottoman law promulgated by Osman Hamdi Bey.

Bell's aim was twofold: to promote archaeological research and to prevent looting at the sites, which foreign archaeologists would guard. It is also clear that Iraqi law assured the possibility of implementing both European and American collections. Hence, Sati' al-Husri, who was Assistant Minister for Education and very close to King Faisal I, expressed some reservations about Bell's law, although Iraqi authorities never complained about how the finds were divided, at least during Bell's lifetime (Baram 1994: 282–3).

King Faisal I of Iraq was present at the official opening of the National Museum in 1926, but in those years neither he nor his ministers made any political use of the Mesopotamian heritage. In Egypt, on the other hand, the opening of Tutankhamen's tomb in 1924 symbolically coincided with the first day of the new Egyptian Parliament, although Egypt eventually abandoned the 'Pharaonic identity', preferring instead to emphasize the Arab identity (Rothfield 2009: 9). Meanwhile, in Turkey, Atatürk began to promote the formation of an artificial national identity and reckoned that the roots of modern Turkey could be found in the ancient Hittite civilization, which had already been discovered in that period (Atakuman 2008).

It was not until 1930 that the Mesopotamian archaeological heritage became part of the curriculum in Iraqi high schools, which gradually contributed to the spread of knowledge on ancient civilizations among the young generation. Al-Husri became the Director of Antiquities in 1934 and expanded the horizons of Iraqi heritage to include Islamic antiquities. He supervised the archaeological investigations at the ruins of the Abbasid Palace in Baghdad and excavated the imposing site of al-Ukhaydir. Hence, he succeeded in portraying both the ancient Mesopotamian civilizations and the Islamic past as the roots of Iraqi heritage and tradition (Baram 1994: 290–3).

The guide to the Iraq Museum, published in 1942, presented an image of Iraq that, for the first time, encompassed four millennia; Faisal I (1883–1933), the first king of Iraq, was included alongside the principal Mesopotamian rulers, such as Naram Sin of Akkad and Hammurabi of Babylon. Undoubtedly, the emphasis on Iraq's ancient past must have had an influence on the boys attending school in the 1940s, among them Saddam Hussein, who was born in 1937 (Baram 1994: 296–9).

When Iraq's Ba'ath Party took over in 1968, the fascination with Mesopotamian antiquities affected the entire political elite. The new National Museum had just opened in 1967, and in 1974 a new Law of Antiquities came into effect to prohibit the export of any antiquities. The identity of Iraq was no longer pan-Arab, but became Iraqi only, and this meant a mixture of Mesopotamian and Islamic traditions that was unique to Iraq. This identity did not coincide with any one of the different components of Iraqi society, namely Sunnis, Shiites and Kurds, but combined them all. Furthermore, the identification of Saddam with Nebuchadnezzar II, who deported the Jews into Babylon, stressed the role played by Iraq in the resistance against Israel. Lastly, the fact that ancient Mesopotamian empires had once ruled enormous territories could have been used to justify Saddam's ambition to be the leader of the Arabs and to expand his power over the bordering regions (Baram 1994).

Saddam severely repressed any looting activity in Iraq, especially in the 1990s, when archaeological sites in the south started to be pillaged after the draining of the marshes had impoverished the inhabitants of these regions (Rothfield 2009: 12–9).

The identification of Saddam and his party with the heritage of Mesopotamia is one of the reasons why the inhabitants of Baghdad sacked the National Museum in April 2003, immediately after the collapse of the Ba'athist regime. As is well known, although it was foreseeable that the museum would be looted, it was not protected by the US Army. Three different bands of thieves appear to have been involved in the looting of the museum from 8–12 April. Several museum pieces were stolen, although far fewer than the media reported; these included masterworks such as the Vase of Warka, the Golden Harp from Ur and the Mask of Warka, as well as a large number of seals, cuneiform tablets and small objects (Gibson 2008). We have US Colonel Matthew Bogdanos, who was appointed to command the multi-task-force agency, to thank not only for finding many of these treasures, such as the aforementioned artefacts, but also for his exhaustive presentation of the events related to the sacking of the museum as well as to the task-force activities (Bogdanos 2005).

The sacking of the National Museum, albeit a dramatic event, caused less damage to Iraq's heritage when compared with the systematic looting at archaeological sites scattered throughout the territory of Iraq. In the beginning, there were many reasons that people turned to looting. As previously mentioned, in some cases it was a manifestation of people's anger against the Ba'athist party, but it was mostly terrible impoverishment that led many people to steal anything that might be of value. Later, looting also became something of a profession, mostly in the southern part of Iraq, where the pillaging of the Sumerian cities had already begun. The complete lack of control in this area of the country, which was a 'no-fly zone', and the impunity that the fall of Saddam's regime seemed to guarantee to thieves, allowed organized teams of looters to excavate the main ancient sites (Palumbo 2005).

Elisabeth Stone, a Stony Brook University professor, started a survey in the southern part of Iraq in 2003. Together with two of her American colleagues and with the logistical assistance of the Italian Carabinieri, Stone flew over the southern territories of Iraq and took pictures of the major archaeological sites. Her work is still in progress, and the database that holds all the available information gives a clear picture not only of the damaged sites, but also of the chronology of looting, as well as the items looted. Fortunately, the looting has decreased somewhat, although many sites continue to suffer damage. Clandestine diggers now seem to prefer larger sites, which can offer artefacts dating to the Ur III and Old Babylonian times; in fact, cuneiform tablets can be found at these sites, and we know that clay tablets have become more widely available on the market. Presumably, this is due to the fact that cuneiform documents cannot be easily faked and are lightweight (Stone 2008a, 2008b, 2015; Matthiae 2015: 100–3).

The most recent damage to the archaeological patrimony of Iraq was carried out by Islamic State of Iraq and Syria (ISIS), with its systematic destruction of sites such as Nimrud, Nineveh and Hatra, as well as at the Mosul Museum. ISIS, which aimed at the construction of an Islamic caliphate, wanted to erase nationalist cultures, traditions and heritage. The attacks on the archaeological heritage were part of a programme intended to annihilate cultural and religious diversity, and at the same time to destroy all pre-Islamic antiquities, which were considered a symbol of western colonialism as well as a reminder of the specific Iraqi identity (Turku 2018: 67–97, Cuneo and Danti 2019). The effect of Nimrud's devastation on the local population can be summarized in the words of Sheikh Khalid al-Jabouri, who was part of a tribal militia in the region of Mosul. He affirmed that Nimrud was part of his life, and a symbol of the whole of Iraq; in other words, he would have preferred to see his own house destroyed, rather than see the devastation of the Neo-Assyrian capital (Turku 2018: 83).

The dissemination of spectacular pictures and videos showing the destructive activities of ISIS was intended to impress both Islamic and western countries, and to demonstrate the invincible power of the ISIS army (Harmanşah 2015). Nevertheless, the demand in the market for Mesopotamian antiquities had become a very good business for ISIS, and the profits derived from this market were the second most important financial resource for the organization, the first being oil revenues (Turku 2018: 49–52).

The Italian politician Francesco Rutelli, who is the president of the association Incontro di Civiltà, recently promoted the reconstruction of one of the human-headed winged bulls destroyed by ISIS at Nimrud. This magnificent sculpture was replicated using a 3D printer. The well-known Italian archaeologist Paolo Matthiae supervised the entire reconstruction process and thus assured the accuracy of the scientific details. The reconstructed bull was then put on display in Rome at the Colosseum and afterward at the UNESCO Palace in Paris. This sculpture is, indeed, a symbol of the indestructibility of culture, art and heritage despite the attacks by ISIS.

3.2 The Carabinieri's contribution

The Carabinieri Corps, Italy's military force and gendarmerie, have participated in missions in countries such as El Salvador, Cambodia, Somalia, Lebanon and Afghanistan, among others (Rush and Benedettini Millington 2015). The Carabinieri were the first task force to arrive in Iraq, and in 2003 started the project to protect the Iraqi heritage; in fact, they were among the very first members of the coalition who realized that the preservation of cultural heritage would have a positive social impact on Iraqi communities (Russel 2008). The protection of cultural patrimony is an important tool in the process of peace-keeping in post-conflict situations (Foradori and Rosa 2017). The so-called 'military archaeology', which has nothing to do with the 'colonial archaeology' of past centuries, can play a significant role in salvaging the archaeological heritage in war-torn countries (Hamilakis 2009).

After the UNESCO conference held in Lyon in May 2003, Carabinieri experts were dispatched to Baghdad, where they collaborated with the Italian Centro Ricerche Archeologiche e Scavi di Torino per il Medio Oriente e l'Asia (CRAST) and the Iraqi State Board of Antiquities and Heritages (SBAH) to set up a database for the stolen pieces, which included pictures, to be sent to Interpol. The operation Antica Babilonia, which started in July 2003, was part of the UNESCO peace-keeping mission. The Carabinieri worked in the province of Nasiriyah and gave assistance to the SBAH. The most important goal of their mission was to suppress illicit excavations, and to document all damage to archaeological sites. The most significant successes against clandestine excavations were the result of helicopter raids; in fact, illicit diggers could easily be located upon the arrival of the helicopters, which scared them away from the archaeological sites where they were working, and in some cases prevented them from continuing their activities. By the time the Antica Babilonia operation was completed, after twenty-four helicopter missions, the Carabinieri had listed many archaeological sites, recovered a huge number of artefacts and arrested several looters (Rush and Benedettini Millington 2015: 161–70).

The Carabinieri operation had the full support of Ambassador Mario Bondioli Osio, whom the coalition provisional authority had appointed Senior Advisor for Culture. He planned to provide trained Iraqi guards to cover all the territory of Dhi-Qar. In 2006, Bondioli Osio was able to put several vehicles at the disposal of the SBAH, as well as police radio base stations, representing the first step in the process of stopping the looting (Russell 2008).

In November 2015 the 38th UNESCO General Conference in Paris established the Blue Helmets for Culture. Afterwards, the Italian government signed an agreement with UNESCO to set up an Italian task force that would collaborate in the peace-keeping projects and help protect the cultural heritage. The Carabinieri Command for the Protection of Cultural Heritage (Comando Carabinieri Tutela Patrimonio Culturale) was part of this task force (Foradori and Rosa 2017).

3.3 The renovation of the Iraq Museum

CRAST's primary commitment in recent years has been the renovation of the Iraq National Museum in Baghdad after its destruction in 2003. CRAST has a long tradition of working in Iraq and collaborating with the SBAH; when CRAST was founded in 1963, it began archaeological excavations in Mesopotamia, at Seleucia and later at several other sites. CRAST also took part in the international projects promoted by the SBAH; these aimed at saving archaeological sites that otherwise would have been submerged in the building of artificial basins and dams, such as the Harmin dam, the Eski Mosul dam and the Kifrin project. The activities in Iraq were co-ordinated by two Italian–Iraqi institutes founded by CRAST, namely the Institute of Archaeological Sciences and the Centre for the Restoration of Monuments.

In collaboration with the SBAH and the Central Restoration Institute (Italian Ministry of Cultural Heritage, MIBACT), CRAST began a documentation project at Nineveh in 2002 intended to verify the state of conservation at the magnificent palace built by the Neo-Assyrian king Sennacherib at Nineveh. Unfortunately, the dramatic events of the following year prevented the work from proceeding; nonetheless, photographer Angelo Rubino did take pictures of the reliefs and these photographs offer the most complete documentation on the decoration of Sennacherib Palace, which unfortunately was completely destroyed by ISIS. In consideration of the cultural importance of these documents, CRAST has exhibited Rubino's photographs in several locations in recent years (Archivio di Stato-Turin, 2007; University Ca' Foscari-Venice, 2015; Martin von Wagner Museum-Würzburg, 2017; University of Pavia-Pavia, 2017; Fondazione Museo Egizio-Turin, 2018).

In 2000–02 CRAST, in co-operation with the Carabinieri, took part in the Bureau for the Recovery of the Iraqi Looted Antiquities (BRILA), and created a database of objects that had been looted from Iraqi regional museums up to 2002. Furthermore, CRAST has co-organized training courses in Amman (2004–05) to teach emergency restoration methods to the Iraqi employees of the SBAH (Menegazzi 2005).

Although the museum had been destroyed, Italian Ambassador Piero Cordone decided that a sign of the possible rebirth of the Iraqi collections would be politically and culturally significant. Hence, in July 2003 he promoted the exhibition of the treasures discovered in the royal graves at Nimrud. These masterpieces remained on display for only one day, but the exhibition demonstrated that the international efforts were directed not only at recovering the stolen artefacts, but also at reopening the museum (Fales 2004: 372).

In consideration of the many years of collaboration between the SBAH and CRAST, the latter institution was asked to submit a proposal for the renovation of the Iraq Museum in Baghdad. The project began in 2006 and was funded by the Italian Ministry of Foreign Affairs and International Cooperation (MAECI), the MIBACT and the Fondazione Banca Nazionale delle Comunicazioni. A strict and productive co-operation with the aforementioned Central Restoration Institute also made possible the restoration of damaged artefacts, such as the Warka Mask, the Warka Vase, the terracotta lions from Tell Harmal and many other Mesopotamian masterpieces. The renovation project was initially co-ordinated by Antonio Invernizzi, and then by Carlo Lippolis, but all the collaborators of CRAST contributed as well.

The first project (2004–08) involved the Great Assyrian Gallery and the Islamic Gallery. The former gallery housed the monumental Neo-Assyrian sculptures and reliefs, which could not be moved. Hence, museum staff had protected them by means of foam padding and sandbags when the political situation became very dangerous at the beginning of 2003. The latter gallery housed masterpieces from Samarra, Mosul and other sites. The Italian architect Roberto Parapetti, who is a collaborator of CRAST as well as President of the Monumenta Orientalia association, directed the renovation of these two galleries with the co-operation of Gianluca Capri. The second and more recent project concerned the Middle Assyrian Gallery and Arch. Parapetti was also responsible for setting up this gallery. When the work was completed on this space, the Iraq Museum was officially reopened, on 28 February 2015. The renovation of the museum involved the lighting of the galleries, new display cases and some architectonical structures such as the arch over the two human-headed winged bulls; this structure aims to give an idea of how these two monumental sculptures appeared in their original location in the palace of King Sargon II in Khorsabad.

One of the main challenges that CRAST faced was how to provide a new way of telling the story of Mesopotamian heritage and the artefacts that are displayed in the museum. As already mentioned, Saddam's regime had manipulated the presentation of Iraq's past for political purposes; hence, it was necessary to build a new consciousness of the universal value of Iraq's cultural patrimony, one that had nothing to do with the previous Ba'athist propaganda. The narrative should be scientifically correct, extremely clear and differentiated according to the age and cultural level of the visitors.

First of all, we represented the longue durée of the ancient Mesopotamian tradition in graphic form; we argued that a visual medium would be more effective than written texts, and hence the whole history of Mesopotamia is summarized and shown on a translucent and backlit Perspex panel that is 4.74 metres long, located in the Middle Assyrian Gallery. Furthermore, the panel, written in English and Arabic, gives more information on the history and art of ancient Iraq. Lastly, a set of drawers displays pictures, each with a printed text. The topics dealt with concern aspects of daily life in ancient Mesopotamia, and are mainly for younger visitors (Lippolis et al. 2016).

More recently, in order to develop children's interest in Iraqi heritage, CRAST has commissioned the publication of comics on both the Mesopotamian cultures and the museum collections. The authors of these comics are Mirko Furlanetto and Laura De Stefani, and the publication and distribution of the first three volumes were sponsored by CRAST as well as by the University of Bologna. In this way, children can easily learn about the history of the Sumerians, Babylonians and Assyrians, and at the same time become aware of the value and vulnerability of Iraq's heritage and the need to protect it, especially from the looting of the archaeological sites.

In 2011, the Monumenta Orientalia association submitted a proposal to the Iraqi government for the reconstruction of the prayer hall at the medieval Madrasa al-Mirjaniya, considered one of the masterpieces of Islamic architecture. Some fragments from the lost building were previously on display in the Iraq Museum, but a new, complete arrangement of these fragments was required. Parapetti was responsible for the renovation project, which was completed in co-operation with CRAST. The reconstructed prayer hall is located in the north court of the museum, near the Islamic Gallery (Parapetti 2017).

3.4 Training courses

The two Italian–Iraqi institutes established in 1969 by CRAST in co-operation with the Iraqi authorities have already been mentioned. In the beginning these were housed in Baghdad in a building designed by the Italian architect Andrea Bruno; after the building was expropriated in 1974, CRAST rented another space in Zuwiya quarter, which it inhabited until 1984. Afterwards the two institutes found a new site in Haifa Street, where they remained until 1999. The next location of the institutes was in Bet al-Galiani, but unfortunately this site was destroyed in the general devastation of all the official buildings in 2003 (Parapetti 2012). The Iraqi government then offered an ancient building in the old centre of Baghdad, and the Italian Ministry for Foreign Affairs sponsored its renovation. The institutes are now active again, and CRAST organizes training courses on cultural heritage, museology and communication at this location.

Furthermore, from 2016 the Carabinieri Italian Task Force Unity for Heritage (U4H) began offering training courses for Iraqi officials. In 2018 two units were established in Iraq – one in Baghdad and the other in Erbil – to provide support to the UNESCO offices in these cities, and to other Iraqi and foreign institutions that work for the protection of local cultural heritage. Around 800 members of the Iraqi police corps have been trained by the U4H to date; moreover, employees of the Tourism and Antiquity Security Directorate of Iraq and of the SBAH have improved their skills thanks to the courses on cultural heritage protection held in Baghdad.

Last but not least, Nicolò Marchetti, from the University of Bologna, is the principal investigator on the project 'Education and Cultural Heritage Enhancement for Social Cohesion in Iraq' (EDUU). This three-year project, which began in 2017, is funded by the European Union. It also involves four other partners, namely CRAST and the universities of Baghdad, Qadisyah and

Kufa. This project aims to spread knowledge of the multi-ethnic, multi-linguistic and multi-cultural traditions of Iraq, and hence to enhance the pluralism of Iraqi civil society. Courses are taught mainly to SBAH employees, but also to school students, and include museology, Near Eastern archaeology, public archaeology, technological skills, international legislation for the protection of cultural heritage and English language for archaeology.

References

Al-Aswad, Hikmat Basheer (2017), 'Nineveh and the City of Mosul', in Lucas P. Petit and Daniele Morandi Bonacossi, eds, *Nineveh, The Great City. Symbol of Beauty and Power*, Leiden, Sidestone Press, p. 260–264

Atakuman, Çiğdem (2008), 'Cradle or Crucible: Anatolia and Archaeology in the Early Years of the Turkish Republic (1923–1938)', in *Journal of Social Archaeology*, Vol. 8, No. 2, p. 214–235

Baram, Amatzia (1994), 'A Case of Imported Identity: The Modernizing Secular Ruling Elites of Iraq and the Concept of Mesopotamian-Inspired Territorial Nationalism, 1922–1992', in *Poetics Today*, Vol. 15, No. 2 (Summer), p. 279–319

Bogdanos, Matthew (2005), 'The Casualities of War: The Truth About the Iraq Museum', in *American Journal of Archaeology*, Vol. 109, No. 3 (July), p. 477–526

Cuneo, Allison E. and Michael D. Danti (2019), 'Tracking Heritage Loss in the Midst of Armed Conflict', in Julie Bessenay-Prolonge, Jean-Jacques Herr and Mathilde Mura, eds, *Archéologie des conflit/Archéologie en conflit. Documenter la destruction au Moyen-Orient et en Asie Centrale...*, Paris, Routes de l'Orient, Actes 2, p. 265–284, https://rdorient.hypotheses.org/category/archeologie-des-conflits-archaeology-of-conflict

Dogde, Toby (2003), *Inventing Iraq. The Failure of Nation Building and a History Denied*, New York, Columbia University Press

Fales, Frederick Mario (2004), *Saccheggio in Mesopotamia. Il museo di Baghdad dalla nascita dell'Iraq a oggi*, Udine, Forum

Foradori, Paolo and Paolo Rosa (2017), 'Expanding the Peacekeeping Agenda. The Protection of Cultural Heritage in War-Torn Societies', in *Global Change, Peace & Security*, Vol. 29, No. 2, p. 145–160

Gibson, McGuire (2008), 'The Looting of the Iraq Museum in Context', in Geoff Emberling and Katharin Hanson, eds, *Catastrophe! The Looting and Destruction of Iraq's Past*, Chicago, The Oriental Institute Museum of the University of Chicago, p. 13–27, https://oi.uchicago.edu/node/3286

Hamilakis, Yannis (2009), 'The "War of Terror" and the Military-Archaeology Complex: Iraq, Ethics and Neo-Colonialism', in *Archaeologies*, Vol. 5, No. 1 (April), p. 39–65

Harmanşah, Ömür (2015), 'ISIS, Heritage, and the Spectacles of Destruction in the Global Media', in *Near Eastern Archaeology*, Vol. 78, No. 3 (September), p. 170–177

Kamel, Lorenzo (2019), *The Middle East from Empire to Sealed Identities*, Edinburgh, Edinburgh University Press

Lippolis, Carlo et al. (2016), *L'Iraq Museum di Baghdad. Gli interventi italiani per la riqualificazione di un patrimonio dell'umanità*, Firenze, Apice

Matthiae, Paolo (2015), *Distruzioni, saccheggi e rinascite. Gli attacchi al patrimonio artistico dall'antichità all'Isis*, Milano, Mondadori Electa

Menegazzi, Roberta, ed. (2005), *An Endangered Cultural Heritage. Iraqi Antiquities Recovered in Jordan*, Firenze, Le Lettere

Nuri, Nahar Muhammed (2018), 'Iraq Is Not Artificial: Iraqi Trends and the Refutation of the Artificial State Hypothesis', in *AlMuntaqa*, Vol. 1 (December), No. 3, p. 9–39, https://doi.org/10.31430/almuntaqa.1.3.0009

Palumbo, Gaetano (2005), 'The State of Iraq's Cultural Heritage in the Aftermath of the 2003 War', in *The Brown Journal of World Affairs*, Vol. 12, No. 1 (Summer), p. 225–238

Parapetti, Roberto (2012), 'The Site of the Italian-Iraqi Institutes of Baghdad, 1969–2010: Migration Chronicle', in *Mesopotamia*, Vol. 47, p. 139–143

Parapetti (2017), 'The Lost Mirjaniya Madrasa of Baghdad: Reconstructions and Additional Notes', in *Mesopotamia*, Vol. 52, p. 173–212

Rothfield, Lawrence (2009), *The Rape of Mesopotamia. Behind the Looting of the Iraq Museum*, Chicago, University of Chicago Press

Rush, Laurie and Luisa Benedettini Millington (2015), *The Carabinieri Command for the Protection of Cultural Property*, Woodbridge, The Boydell Press

Russel, John M. (2008), 'Efforts to Protect Archaeological Sites and Monuments in Iraq, 2003–2004', in Geoff Emberling and Katharin Hanson, eds, *Catastrophe! The Looting and Destruction of Iraq's Past*, Chicago, The Oriental Institute Museum of the University of Chicago, p. 29–43, https://oi.uchicago.edu/node/3286

Stone, Elizabeth C. (2008a), 'Archaeological Site Looting: The Destruction of Cultural Heritage in Southern Iraq', in Geoff Emberling and Katharin Hanson, eds, *Catastrophe! The Looting and Destruction of Iraq's Past*, Chicago, The Oriental Institute Museum of the University of Chicago, p. 65–80, https://oi.uchicago.edu/node/3286

Stone, Elizabeth C. (2008b), 'Patterns of Looting in Southern Iraq', in Antiquity, Vol. 82, No. 315 (March), p. 125–138

Stone, Elizabeth C. (2015), 'An Update on the Looting of Archaeological Sites in Iraq, in *Near Eastern Archaeology*, Vol. 78, No. 3 (September), p. 178–186

Turku, Helga (2018), *The Destruction of Cultural Property as a Weapon of War. ISIS in Syria and Iraq*, Cham, Palgrave Macmillan

Omar Mohammed

Chapter 4: Space, Time and People: How the Destruction of Mosul's Heritage Is Reshaping Its People's Future

> A man sets out to draw the world. As the years go by, he peoples a space with images of provinces, kingdoms, mountains, bays, ships, islands, fishes, rooms, instruments, stars, horses, and individuals. A short time before he dies, he discovers that the patient labyrinth of lines traces the lineaments of his own face.
>
> *Borges (2004: 183)*

> How does an ethnographer [historian] write about violence [against the history of his own city]? How can he make sense of violent acts, for himself and for his readers, without compromising its sheer excess and its meaning-defying core? How can he remain a scholarly observer when the country of his birth is engulfed by terror?

These were the questions raised by Errol Valentine Daniel (1996) in his book *Charred Lullabies*. His words seemed meaningful to me while I was writing this chapter. It is almost impossible to make sense of the events that have occurred in Mosul in recent years, but I will nonetheless try to shed light on the history of violence against space and time.

For centuries, Mosul created and maintained a unique cultural identity. It has endured periods of bloodshed and extreme change in its structure, rule and architecture. Any other city may have given way to what might have been a completely new system and social fabric after every foreign invasion.

The city of Mosul has experienced almost 300 invasions by various foreign nations and empires. Nevertheless, it has always protected its cultural heritage and identity, whether through language, literature or visual memory. Since its destruction by the so-called Islamic State of Iraq and Syria (ISIS), much research has focused on its tangible heritage without taking into account its role in shaping the local identity. Space is the context through which we can examine the formation of time and ideas, or as my title implies, people and time. Arguably, history works when people can engage daily with their inherited surroundings (Urry

1995). The recent invasion by ISIS and its subsequent defeat have left the city with staggering losses of both tangible and intangible heritage. Furthermore, we have seen, since this destruction occurred, hundreds of articles treating and discussing culture as a material object disconnected from its main function of producing the city's identity.

This chapter aims to explore the ties between cultural heritage and cultural identity and their effect on Mosul's future by examining the urban space, time and people. It will provide examples of the city's cultural heritage and demolished historical sites and the discussions they have triggered in the city since the ISIS occupation. While Mosul is known for its cultural diversity – from its ancient history to its early Christian presence, and its Jewish and Islamic heritage – this chapter will focus on the Islamic heritage as its case study; however, this focus is in no way intended to ignore or downplay other aspects of its culture and history.

The conceptual formation of the social fabric and heritage of any old city, and specifically of Mosul, with its hundreds of visible sites representing different historical periods, can be understood through various factors: the urban structure of its space; the connection between the urban structure and the historical narratives on how the space was created (Khoury 1997; Tabbaa 1982); the interaction among its inhabitants, their daily lives and the visual memory they have established through various factors and activities that have shaped – on several bases – the narrative of their past and present; and the language, which significantly influences the formation of the historical story regarding space, time and people. Language becomes the main factor for understanding the development of heritage and its place in the people's visual memory and historical narrative. Major historical works may not give us a clear understanding of Mosul's cultural heritage; everyday proverbs tell us how the people engage with their heritage. Since this chapter does not address the role of the linguistic heritage of Mosul, the author will only use that indicator to explain the connection between space and people in relation to cultural heritage.

4.1 Religion and urban structure

To understand the urban structure of post-ISIS Mosul, we should first explore ISIS's role in the formation of the historical and social narrative of the city. We need to know as well the conceptual and contextual justifications that ISIS used to legitimize its destruction of Mosul's cultural heritage. ISIS announced its goals in advance, citing a document based on a verdict by a Yemeni scholar named

Muhammad ash-Shawkani (1759–1839).[1] However, the main question should not be whether ISIS adopted an Islamic perspective that viewed the whole cultural heritage as a form of idolatry. Instead we should try to understand why ISIS chose to systematically destroy Mosul's historical sites, and from which historical narrative they viewed the city and its urban structure.

Mosul's sophisticated urban space has undergone several transformations during its long history. The city is known as 'The City of Prophets' for having been the residence of a number of prophets. It is also known as 'The Mother of All Mosques'. The city's structure formalized its cultural identity during the period of Ottoman rule, particularly under the Jalili family. During that time, the *Waqf* (endowment) became an expression of power. The Jalili family endowments still make up almost 70 per cent of the historical sites of Old Mosul (Dewachi 1963). The city experienced rapid growth through the building of religious institutions such as mosques, schools and law courts. When we look at the map of Old Mosul, we can quickly see how the increasing number of such buildings was related to the economic and political control of the leading families. It became a tradition in the city to surround a religious building with suqs and khans (Yahya 2012). In the following paragraphs, I will cite an example to show the connection between identity, heritage and economy in the process of shaping Mosul's cultural heritage.

The history of the city, home to more than 600 mosques and shrines, is deeply rooted in the Islamic narrative that ISIS confronted. Once it had occupied the city in 2014, ISIS began to carry out the systematic destruction of Mosul's identity. First of all, its leaders forced the city's non-Muslim inhabitants to flee, destroying their monuments to remove their heritage from the city's history. Then came the destruction of its ancient Assyrian monuments and cultural sites. After this brutality against Mosul's non-Islamic past, the invaders turned to the Muslim community; they began systematically to destroy Islamic archaeological sites, as well as museums, libraries and manuscripts. They also took aim at Mosul's linguistic heritage. Where the city once had a rich, peaceful vocabulary of everyday words and phrases, the group implemented a vocabulary of violence and social division – their own medieval vocabulary. We began to hear *diwan* instead of *wizara* (ministry), *hisba* instead of *shurta* (police), *Bayt al-mal* (house

---

1 His fatwa is known as '*Mashru'yaat hadm al adhriha wa al qubur*' (The legitimacy of demolishing Shrines and tombs in [Islam]) was reproduced and reprinted by ISIS in Mosul three days after they began destroying the historical sites of the city in August 2014.

of money) instead of *al-Bank al-Markazi* (central bank). New labels were applied to the social classes: *ansar* (helpers) were the 'local' ISIS members and fighters; *muhajirun* (immigrants) were the ISIS foreign fighters; and *munasirun* (allies) were those non-members who supported and welcomed ISIS. Opponents of ISIS who were jihadists were called *mukhalifun* (transgressors). Finally, *āmma* (commoners) were the lower classes who opposed ISIS (Mohammed 2018).

4.2 An impenetrable urban space: the destruction and reconstruction of Al-Nuri Mosque

Opinions vary regarding the destruction of al-Hadbaa minaret, its importance and the importance of the Old City of Mosul, in which ISIS's last military operations led to its destruction. Some say there is no significant value in the old town, claiming that it is only a tiny portion of Mosul's total area. This is true, geographically speaking. Others have belittled the minaret's significance, saying foolishly and awkwardly that it was 'odd-looking', that Mosulis did not know it and that there were no real ties that bound them to it. Others have related the Great Mosque of Al-Nuri to the Crusades and to Nur al-Din Zenki's campaigns against the Crusaders and the Fatimids, while still others have tried to give the impression that the Iraqi military (which consists mostly of Shiites) would have to die on its stony steps to liberate it from ISIS.[2]

It is, therefore, important to explore the role played by the old city's historical icons in shaping its people's cultural identity. This is an attempt to demonstrate and understand Mosul and its cultural heritage. To this end, I am writing in two capacities: as an historian as well as a native who grew up in the city and witnessed it before, during and after its occupation by ISIS – observing every post-2003 event and development. It is in an attempt to liberate Mosul and its heritage from the misconceptions and factual errors that have arisen and to restore the real and genuine value of the old city's culture, history and society.[3] This chapter will

2 See for example a controversial article on the Hadbaa and its connection to the people by Rasha al-Aqeedi (2017), who criticizes how the people of Mosul remembered the Hadbaa.

3 Conflicts over the narrative of the origin of Al-Nuri Mosque were sparked on social media between Iraqis, many of whom claimed the mosque was originally built on a demolished church, which triggered controversial religious arguments. Others saw the destruction of the mosque as a positive symbol of the defeat of ISIS and used it in sectarian discourse. Still others thought that the mosque had not been destroyed by ISIS, but rather by the Iraqi security forces to take revenge on Mosul and its people. All these controversial arguments still exist in the discourse of many Iraqi people, but it is

provide a list of the irreplaceable historical sites, markets, schools and ruins that were destroyed during the military operations.

History serves to resolve the complex obscurities that we encounter in reading about current events, not to make them more complicated and obscure. Since Abu Bakr al-Baghdadi's declaration of his self-proclaimed caliphate at Al-Nuri Grand Mosque, so-called experts have produced tens of studies, research papers, journalistic reports, theories and opinions.

Firstly, it has been argued that al-Baghdadi's motive in choosing Al-Nuri Mosque to announce his caliphate was due to its relationship to Nur al-Din Zenki, who led several campaigns against the Crusaders. This is an argument that al-Baghdadi himself used. Furthermore, there are those who continue to refer to the eternal clash of civilizations between the East and the West. They derive their ideas from Edward Said (1977), who shed light on the East–West conflict in his book *Orientalism*, who expanded the role of journalism to one of passing historical judgments as facts and lost their ability to distinguish between 'journalism' and 'history' because of the enormous volume of data available on the World Wide Web. Moreover, and worse still, they generated historical misconceptions about Mosul that went viral and started to propound erroneous theories about Mosul and its heritage and society (motivated by their quest for self-advancement and other aims).

The jihadi groups always use Nur al-Din Zenki's name in connection with his victories against the Crusaders and the Assassins (see for example Elisséeff 1995; Raby 2004). Their weaponization of history has served mainly to convince the youth to relate to them and espouse their historical doctrines. This reception of jihadist rhetoric about Zenki and Mosul was misguided, however.

This chapter will attempt to disengage Nur al-Din Zenki from Al-Nuri Grand Mosque and to reaffirm the historical facts. Al-Nuri Grand Mosque was not built on religious or sectarian bases, as many propound, it rather served as a new symbol of the new regime in Mosul. The great mosque has played a fundamental role in shaping Mosul's cultural identity. ISIS's employment of the mosque does not necessarily make the Mosulis and their attachment to the mosque and its minaret responsible for the rise of ISIS. The minaret served Mosul as a symbol of perseverance and survival, with historical roots in the Mosuli psyche.

---

important to note that they appear mostly in the young generation's discourse rather than in educated and academic or official discourse.

In this regard, the Mosuli historian Ahmad Qasim Jum'a,[4] who spent forty years studying the history and blueprints of Al-Nuri Grand Mosque, said in an interview: 'When a Mosuli says "I am the son of Al-Hadbaa", and if you were to get the stones to speak, they would have addressed bold speeches and given significant meanings to the Minaret and the Mosque.' The mosque and minaret are located in the heart of Mosul's markets, and they have a pure Mosuli identity. Over time, the mosque became a beacon fostering various types of knowledge and literature, such as geology, architecture and pure science. It is like a crystal. Once it is illuminated, it scintillates with Mosul's heritage in the most exquisite detail and is in itself a remarkable architectural marvel.

The story of the construction of the mosque and the minaret defines their urban significance to the Mosulis. History provides vivid details about the moment when the suggestion to build the mosque in Mosul and who was who was behind the idea. Kiatib al-Isfahani (519–579) provides the background on its construction in his book, *Al-Barq al-Shami*:

> The reason for its construction is that there was a large area of ruins at the center of the city, and the rumours spread about it repelled the people from it. There were legends about those ruins that if anyone tried to build on them or cultivate their soil, that person's life would dwindle, and whatever one's goal was, it would never be attained. (Kātib al-Isfahānī 1987)

Ibn al-Athir also tells us about Omar:

> [Nur ad-Din] rode in person to its site and viewed it. He climbed the minaret of the mosque of Abū Hadīr, looked down on the site of his mosque and ordered that the neighbouring houses and shops should be added to the land that he viewed but that nothing should be taken without the willing agreement of the owners. He put the Shaykh 'Umar al-Mallā' in charge of the project, a pious and good man. The properties were purchased from their owners at most substantial prices and the construction began, on which large sums were expended. The building was completed in the year 568 [i.e. AD 1172–3]. (Ibn al-Athīr 2008: 193)

Thus, Mu'in al-Din Omar Al-Mawsili, known as 'Al-Malla'a (died AH 570/AD 1174), the grand shaykh of Mosul, advised him to build the mosque (Ibn al-Athīr 2008: 193). Therefore, the initiative was primarily Al-Malla'a Al-Mawsili's (Kātib al-Isfahānī 1987), and his motive was to inhabit and cultivate this area of ruins. The mosque was not built on top of any house of worship. The mosque was an innovation to revive the city. For most of the mosque's lifespan, it bore the name

4 Phone interview with Ahmed Qasim Jum'a, 13 November 2018. See also his important book (Jum'a 1989).

of al-Malla'a.[5] Ṣibt Ibn Al-Jawzi notes: 'it was called Al-Malla'a by this name because he used to fill clay jars [with water from the river] and lived from day-to-day work and never owned anything' (Mohammed 2017). Al-Malla'a Al-Mawsili had a good reputation in his Mosuli environment. He was also called 'Omar al-Mawla' because he took it upon himself to manage and construct the mosque, and Nur al-Din Zenki assigned the mosque to him. Moreover, Abu Shama (1956), in his book *Al-Rawdatayn fi akhbar al-dawlatayn*, about the events of 566, notes that the first to celebrate the prophet's birth was Al-Malla'a. He used to conduct the celebration annually, in the presence of princes and poets, filled with joy and gladness. Furthermore, Al-Malla'a was the first to advise Nur al-Din Zenki to endow property to the mosque to benefit the city's poor people.

After construction of the mosque was completed, life flourished in the area of the ruins, and Al-Malla'a Al-Mawsili was successful in reviving Mosul. Later, a shrine was built for Al-Malla'a outside the walls of the city on the road to the Tigris river (Dewachi 1963), where people continue to visit his shrine, as Yassin Al-Umari mentions in his book *Muniyat al-udaba'* ('Umarī 1955).[6] Furthermore, there is an alley named after Al-Malla'a honouring Shaykh Omar Al-Malla'a, which was the name used in Mosul referring to Al-Nuri Grand Mosque until the seventeenth century. The mosque was a Mosuli landmark, named after its founder, builder and then its manager. The association with Nur al-Din Zenki was made after studies purported to connect the mosque with Nur al-Din for the sole purpose of relating it to the Crusades, promoting the idea of Islamic warfare against the Crusaders. The minaret's 'crookedness' has been interpreted as an anti-government symbol, whereas in fact its arched shape is an important symbol for Mosulis, as well as the markets that were formed near the mosque. Many crafts and professions were established around it and remain to this day, such as wool weaving, rug-making, blacksmithing and metalworking. The mosque has become a pure Mosuli symbol and is closely linked to Mosul's identity, resulting in its architectural, civic and economic integration and the city's capacity for rebirth and recovery.

---

5 We have few details of the life of Omar bin Muhammed Al-Malla, who was a Shaykh and religious advisor of Nuruddin Zangi and was well respected by the people. More on his life can be found in al-Zarkali (2007). On the architecture of Al-Nuri Mosque see Tabbaa (1982).

6 Yāsīn ibn Khayr Allāh al-Khaṭīb 'Umarī (1745–1819) was an historian from Mosul who authored two books on the history of Mosul; he belonged to the Al-Umari family, the main religious family that served under the Ottoman rule. See his most important book on Mosul: 'Umarī 1974.

The Mosuli archaeologist Amir Al-Jumaili, a professor at the University of Mosul, contends that

> the minaret is a symbol and an identifier of Mosul. Mosulis have always looked at the minaret as their symbol of perseverance. Its existence is coupled with the presence of the Mosulis. Each city has its pigment, and Al-Hadbaa is Mosul's pigment. Whenever we couple Mosul to the Assyrian Nineveh, we use the Assyrian symbols (the Lamassu) with Al-Hadbaa minaret. The Mosulis spent years preserving its architectural style and Mosul's memory. Al-Hadbaa's memory image is not only architectural but also cultural that is coupled with the development of the Mosuli colloquial language and society.[7]

To this, Ahmad Qasim Jum'a adds the following:

> Mosul without Al-Hadbaa is like a body without a heart, and retrieving it is a historical necessity for the world as Al-Hadbaa is not only a Mosuli heritage but also a global one. It is possible to rebuild it in just six months because we have all the blueprints for its structure and embellishments. We handed these blueprints to UNESCO a long time ago. UNESCO's engineering consultant Mohammad Taib Al-Laila (who was killed after his house was bombed during an airstrike on eastern Mosul) redrew the blueprints of Al-Hadbaa, and it is possible to rebuild it in less than eight months if [we have] all the necessary material, tools, and the will to rebuild it.[8]

When Nur al-Din Zenki decided to build the mosque in the twelfth century, the people of Mosul asked many questions regarding Zenki's intentions and whether it would be constructed and financed with the public's money, that is, *Bayt al-Mal* (house of money), or with Zenki's own resources. After the destruction of the mosque in 2017, several meetings were held between archaeologists, historians, architects and the major families of Mosul to discuss the same issues regarding the mosque. It is the continuity of the cultural heritage when space becomes part of the visual memory.

For centuries, Mosulis came to Al-Hadbaa regardless of their religious backgrounds. In Al-Jami' Al-Kabir neighbourhood (formerly Darb Daraj), Muslims and Christians lived side by side and practised their crafts and professions in the area surrounding the mosque (Dewachi 1963). They established their businesses here, in the very heart of Mosul, which the Mosulis call 'Our Old Lady Hadbaa'. Raghad Hammadi, a young woman who lived under ISIS's reign for three years and witnessed every detail of the liberation war, remarks: 'Al-Hadbaa is my identity. She, Hadbaa, is not just brick; she is

7 Interviews conducted at different times with Professor Amir Al-Jumaily, head of the Mosul School of Archaeology, Mosul University, 2017, 2018, 2019.

8 Phone interview with Ahmed Qasim Jum'a, 13 November 2018.

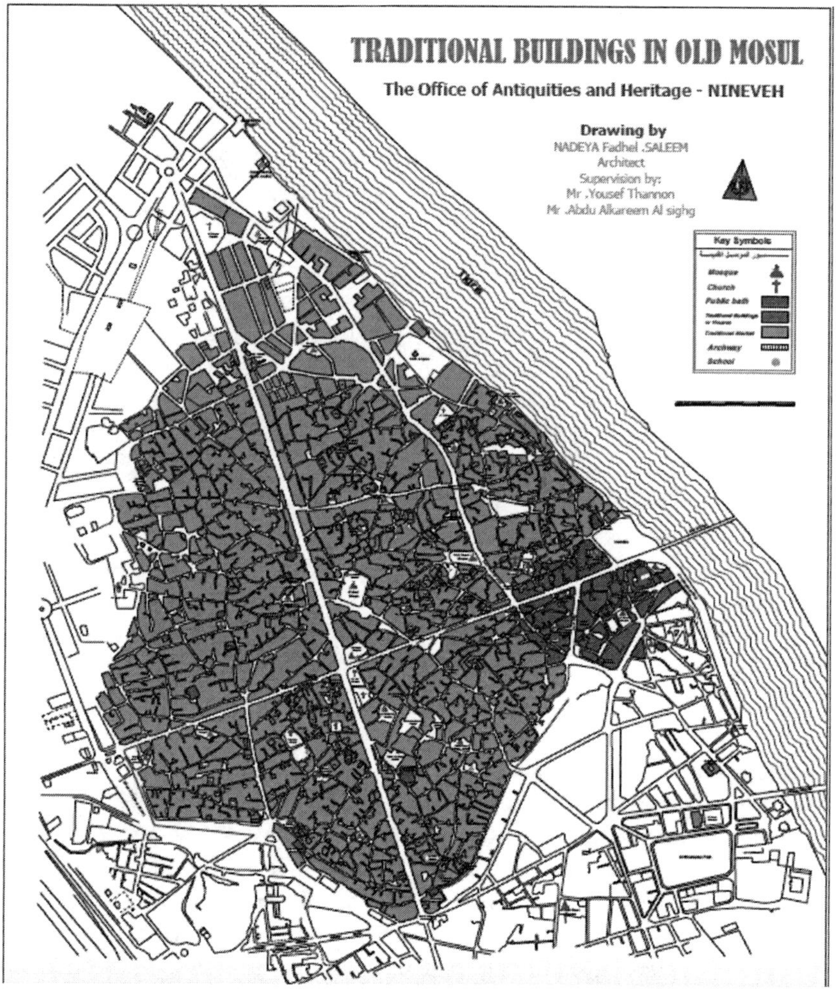

Figure 4.1: Traditional buildings in Old Mosul.

Source: The Office of Antiquities and Heritage – Nineveh (courtesy Saud Al Jalili).

Nineveh's glory and its glorious history. By blowing it up, they stole our symbol with it. The minaret's hunchback is no longer hunched, yet, it is Mosul's back that got hunched.'

4.3 Suqs of Old Mosul: The complexity of time and space

The Old suqs (bazaars) of Mosul, the heart of its social identity, were severely damaged during the battle to retake the city from ISIS. For centuries, the Old Suqs played a crucial role in developing and preserving a socio-economic system that facilitated coexistence in Mosul. It not only served as the economic core of the city, but brought all the different groups of Mosul society together in a very complicated but solid social structure. In the markets, throughout the history of Mosul, Jewish, Christian and Muslim communities lived together and contributed to the shaping of Mosul's identity (Al-Ali Beg 2005). This was also the area where the Mosuli dialect, oral literature and proverbs were created (see Al-Ali Beg 2005; Socin 1847).[9] A brief look at the collection of Mosul's proverbs reveals thousands of proverbs related to the markets.

The Old suqs are located in the south-east quarter of the city, where most of the cultural heritage sites are found, having developed around the medieval markets. The markets' expansion was not just a sign of economic growth in Mosul (Kemp 1979). They played a significant role in the politics of the ruling elites. The vast majority of markets in the Old City were built near a mosque or religious building or a historical site (Al-Hayali 2017). Wich explains the role mosques played in enhancing cultural and economic. Under the Atabegs (Patton 1991), the market area grew considerably and spread north as well as south. After the fall of Mosul to the Mongols in 1262,[10] and throughout the Turkmen era (Qaddawi 2012), economic activity was significantly reduced, and the market area shrank to a small enclave. Such a decline in the market area not only harmed the economy, but also had a significant impact on the cultural life of the city (Qaddawi 2012). After the Ottomans occupied Mosul in 1519 (Khoury 1997: 24, 26–7, 58), the economy of the city once again began to flourish, a trend which continued during the Jalili era; the market then gradually declined after the Ottoman centralization and later during the British Mandate, and after Iraq's independence under Qasim and Saddam. When ISIS occupied Mosul in June 2014, they effected systematic

9 On the proverbs of Mosul see Al-Dabbagh (1956: 21). See also Socin (1847).

10 For more details see Qaddawi (2015).

changes and destroyed the Old suqs, altering their historical identity and casting a shadow over the visual memory of the people.

Mosul's markets had been established and divided by profession. Each market was named after the primary profession practised there. Some markets also took their names from the historical sites that make up the heart of the suq, such as Suq Al Nuri, which refers to the Al-Nuri Mosque. Other markets were connected to *waqfiyyat* (endowments) (Muhammad 2011) or *kuttabs* (elementary schools), or to a particular family that owned the land (Chalabi 1927; Al-Ali Beg 2005). The rise and growth of Mosul's old markets contributed to a very complex identity for the city and its people. Around the markets were the centres of the successive governments of the city. They also served as the political heart where the old and notable families of the city resided. This is also where the oldest churches of the various Christian sects were found, as well as the heart of the Islamic cultural heritage. It is safe to say that the markets of Old Mosul served as the heart of the city's unique coexistence and diversity. However, this diversity was dependent on economic collaboration, which was based on the presence of each group's historical sites. All were merged in the markets to serve their cultural and economic interests.

The social dynamics of Mosul can also be identified in the Old suqs. The markets specialized in producing goods for the middle and upper classes, traders and workers. This diversity constituted a social structure that clearly illustrates how the people of Mosul were associated with their professions. The Great Nuri Mosque is the quarter where the oldest Christian families surrounded the heart of this geographical area, along with government buildings, the Central Bank and the public service administration.

It became a tradition in Mosul for a family to own a small shop in the old markets. Most of the notable families owned – through the endowment system – the old markets; other families and individuals aimed at buying property there in order to identify themselves with the city. This social process of buying property in the Old City played a significant role in the formation of Mosul's social fabric. When the city was destroyed, many families began calculating their losses, not in the outskirts of the city nor the residential areas, but only in the old markets. This process of claiming historical authority is now playing a vital role in the reshaping of the city's identity.

The markets were a locus of economic exchange. They were part of the social and historical dynamic that, besides what was discussed previously, shaped the local perspective on the regional and international culture and heritage (Janabi 1982). The market in Old Mosul used to welcome merchants from other countries as well as from other Iraqi cities (Janabi 1982). It helped to protect the

Figure 4.2: Khan Al Gumrig, reconstruction process.

city's civic and historical identity by its impact on literature, language and history, through interaction between people of different ethnicities and cultures. It also had a significant influence on the architecture of Mosul (Tabbaa 1982; Janabi 1982).

In 2014, when ISIS tried to force the people to reopen their shops in the old markets, the people refused and resisted the order, as they realized that keeping the markets running would legitimize ISIS and its rule, which was relying on the people themselves.[11] This act illustrates how people viewed their heritage and its importance. As a result, most of the local merchants and owners fled the city, in the hope of returning once ISIS was defeated. After the city was liberated in 2017, the merchants went back and found that almost everything they had owned had been destroyed by the international coalition. They again had to emigrate, either to Kurdistan or to the East Bank of Mosul.

Below is a list of the most important destroyed markets in Old Mosul.

- Suq Bab-i Tub (Cannon Gate): This Ottoman suq occupies most of the central area surrounded by the Ottoman administrative buildings. It was the site of most of the traditional markets for middle-class people and also sold second-hand products. ISIS changed the architecture of the suq, destroying and replacing most of its ancient buildings. Moreover, they replaced the suq's main mosque, Al-Sabunji, with a new mosque that they built and named after the former ISIS leader, Abu Bakr al-Baghdadi. The market was heavily damaged during the battle to retake the city from ISIS.[12]
- Suq Haraj: The word *haraj* refers to the nature of the market itself, where lower- and middle-class city-dwellers go to shop, and where people come from rural areas to buy or sell products. The market is known for its disorganized crowds and shops. However, it is surrounded by very old Ottoman khans, *hammams* (bath houses) and markets. It is on the south side of the Bab-i Tub market. ISIS razed the old market to the ground and replaced it with a new market. Consequently, the Suq Haraj has lost its historical value. Later, most of it was damaged during the battle to retake Mosul from ISIS. The importance of this market lies in the interconnections among the people around a historical space.
- Suq Al-Sawwafa (Wool Merchants' Market): This market is located in the heart of the Old suqs. It gave its name to one of the city's notable families, which built its legacy on the wool trade with Britain and India, as well as the religious statue that the Sawwaf family obtained after Muhammed Mahmud Al Sawwaf returned from Egypt in the 1940s and established the second

11 Check Mosul Eye website in the section: *Heritage*, https://mosul-eye.org/category/heritage.

12 The list created by the author is based on documents he collected during his stay in Mosul under ISIS rule.

branch of the Muslim Brotherhood in Mosul (Mohammed 2016). The legacy of these markets maintains the critical connection between the market growth in Mosul and the Jalili family's leadership, when other families began competing for political influence. It also contributed to the development of Mosul's cosmopolitan identity through trade between Mosul and other nations. The people neglected the market after ISIS occupied the city and harmed its cultural life, as many of the livestock owners stopped selling their goods to the city after ISIS seized their sheep and other animals. Rural and urban communities traditionally had found a space for communication in these markets, but once ISIS severed this connection, the market lost its value. It was completely destroyed during the battle to retake the city from ISIS. The Sawwaf family has now moved to Turkey.

- Suq Al-Attarin (Spice Market): This market is of the greatest value in the formation of Mosul's cultural heritage and is fundamentally connected to the beginning of Mosul's development. It is located in the heart of Mosul's Old City, the historic home of the wealthiest families, and is primarily owned by the most influential families, notably al-Jalili. It played a crucial role in putting Mosul on the Silk Road for its trade in spices with China and India. Furthermore, it still holds most of al-Jalilis' *waqfiyyat*. One indication of the market's importance for the wealthy and powerful families of Mosul is that it is located right next to the goldsmiths' market (Suq al-Sagha), where the city's money was minted and held.

The concept of coexistence between different religions and ethnicities did not apply to Mosul's neighbourhoods. The urban structure of neighbourhoods in Old Mosul is based on systematic social division. There are separate neighbourhoods for Christians, Muslims and Jews. Nevertheless, the real diversity, inclusion and coexistence took place in the city's Old suqs, for we can see in the Sagha (Goldsmiths') market multi-ethnic and multi-cultural groups working together in the same place. That was the real value of both the space and the cultural heritage of the suq. Most of the owners and workers in these markets fled after ISIS occupied the city. ISIS also changed the market's architecture and opened within the small alleys new ones that undermined the suq's historical structure. This market also contained what was most important, both religiously and politically: the mosque of the Jalili family, Al-Pasha Mosque, named after Husayn Pasha al-Jalili, the second founder of the Jalili family and the Mosuli ruler who defeated Nadir Shah of Persia when he besieged Mosul in 1743. His legacy became a symbol of the cultural and political identity of Mosul. The mosque was heavily damaged during the battle to retake the city from ISIS. However, shortly after its liberation, the Jalili family and volunteers decided to rebuild the mosque. Its rehabilitation was completed in less than a year. They organized a ceremony to reopen the Al-Pasha Mosque, which is now functioning as a symbol of the resilience of the city and its people.

- Suq Al-Haddadin (Blacksmiths): Located east of Old Mosul, this compound comprises more than ninety shops dating back to the Ottoman era and mostly owned as *awqaf* belonging to the Jalili family. It was the heart of the artisans' area and was always crowded with farmers coming from the countryside to purchase farming tools. The market managed, for a long time, to maintain its Ottoman architecture. However, after 2014, ISIS remodelled most of the shops and did significant damage to the Ottoman style. It was destroyed during the battle to retake the city from ISIS. Volunteers have now partly renovated it with support from the Jalili family.
- Suq Al-Atamih (The Dark Market): This Ottoman market was known for its architectural design, which kept the market dark and protected. It was destroyed during the battle to retake Mosul from ISIS.
- Khan Al-Jumrik (Customs Khan): This market, owned and built by the Jalili family, was Mosul's station on the Silk Road and served as its centre for international trade. Damaged during the battle to retake the city from ISIS, it too has been renovated by the Jalili family.
- Bab-i Saray (The Palace Gate): Named after the old wall of Mosul, this is the Old City's central market and contains Suq Al-Attarin, Al-Sagha, Al-Haddadin, Al-Najjarin and Al-Atamih. Much of it was damaged by ISIS and later during the battle to retake the city.
- Khan Hammu Al Kaddu: This is the only compound in Mosul built by the Al-Kaddu family with two levels in the middle of the eighteenth century, during the Ottoman era. The Khan contained more than 300 shops and rooms for merchants who came to Mosul from other areas and was used by Ottoman officials as a customs office. It was destroyed during the battle to retake Mosul from ISIS. Afterwards it was razed to the ground by the Kaddu family, who decided not to rebuild it. New buildings in a modern architectural style will replace it.

Although ISIS and the international coalition destroyed most of the markets mentioned above, local residents have restored several historic shops. The problem facing the city of Mosul and its cultural heritage is not how many shops can be restored to preserve its cultural identity. Rather, it is the reconstruction strategy, which has so far ignored both the social fabric and the complicated role of the

Figure 4.3: Entrance of Suq Al Haddadin, Blacksmiths, 2019.
Source: Saad Hadi.

market in providing a space where people can communicate. It has also ignored the importance of heritage preservation, as well as its impact on people's visual memory. The international efforts to rebuild Mosul have, due to the planners' lack of understanding of the Old City and its socio-economic fabric, accelerated the decline of this cultural heritage and its ability to protect the future of the city.

4.4 The uncounted destruction: The private libraries and kuttabs (elementary schools)

Mosul, like other Middle Eastern cities, developed and flourished under Islamic rule, where education was at the heart of the state agency. Like many other ancient cities, Mosul had developed, in its early days of transformation under the Islamic rule, an educational system. Although it focused on Islamic education, such as the study of the Quran, Hadith and other aspects of the Sharia, it also fostered a special relationship between education, architecture and cultural development. Thus the city maintained and preserved its intellectual identity.

Beginning in the seventeenth century, Mosul witnessed the emergence of many schools attached to mosques as well as private schools.[13] Despite the need for education, establishing a school in Mosul did not necessarily mean that it was being built to promote knowledge. For the schools' founders, it was an expression of power and influence in the city (Khoury 1997), and a sign of belonging. Families such as the Jalilis and Umaris were at the heart of this competition. This tradition continued and developed through various historical eras. The importance of this system lies not in the number of schools or what they taught, but rather in how such political competition in the cultural heritage space has contributed to the formation of the city's identity. The founder with more space than any other became the most influential for the cultural identity of the city. The role played by schools and private libraries in protecting and preserving the cultural heritage of the city can be understood through their socio-economic impact. Many of these schools and private libraries were funded by the *awqaf* and markets in Old Mosul. They not only served as educational hubs but also produced the meaning of preserving and developing the architecture and visual memory. The tradition of being educated in an old school, where many notable personalities of the city had studied or taught, was an act of belonging to the city.

During the battle to retake the city from ISIS, most of the schools and private libraries in Old Mosul were destroyed or severely damaged such that they cannot be restored. Dozens of articles have discussed the destruction of Old Mosul, but none has mentioned these schools and libraries. Therefore, this chapter documents the destruction. Since there is not enough space to discuss everything about the schools, short descriptions will suffice.[14]

- Ibn Yunis Al Nahawi: Located in Al Shahwan district on the shore of the Tigris river, it was known as Al Zayniyya, which refers to Zayn ad-Din Ali Kutchek, the father of Muzaffar ad-Din Gökböri. It was heavily damaged during the battle to retake Mosul from ISIS. It was completely razed to the ground by the governor of Mosul, Nawfal Al Akkub, who attempted to demolish the entire Old City after its liberation between 2017 and 2018.

---

13 On the emergence of schools in Mosul, Chalabi (1927) provides a unique account of the schools and their role in Mosul. I also relied on his book to make connections between the information I collected during and after ISIS on the schools and the manuscripts.

14 The information was collected and documented by the author since ISIS's occupation of Mosul in 2014. See the appendix for attached photos and maps of the suqs of Old Mosul.

- Al Ahmadiyya: Built by Ahmad Effendi in the sixteenth century, the school held more than 260 rare manuscripts. All the manuscripts, as well as the school itself, were destroyed during the battle to retake Mosul from ISIS.
- Al-Madrasa Al-Islamiyya and its private library: Attached to the Nuri Mosque, which was destroyed by ISIS in July 2017, it contained Mosul's rarest medical manuscripts.
- Al-Aghwat: Attached to the Al-Aghwat Mosque, it was severely damaged during the battle to retake Mosul from ISIS. None of its manuscripts survived. It was built by Ibrahim and his brother Ismail, the sons of the founder of the Jalili family, Abdul Jalil.
- Bab Al-Tub: Built by Abu Al Tutunji in 1815, it has been destroyed.
- Al-Pasha School: This is attached to Al-Pasha Mosque, which was built by Husain Pasha al-Jalili around 1778. It was severely damaged but has been recently renovated by the Jalili family. It held more than 368 manuscripts; all were lost during the battle to retake Mosul from ISIS.
- Bakr Effendi: Located in Ras-i Kur district in Old Mosul, it was built by Yunis Effendi in 1780 and held more than 115 rare manuscripts (Chalabi 1927), all of which were destroyed, along with the school, during the battle for Mosul.
- Jamshid: Built in 1203 and attached to Jamshid Mosque in Old Mosul, it has been destroyed.
- Chuwaichati: Located in Bab-i Jadid, this was one of the oldest schools in Mosul, built in 1494; it was destroyed during the battle for Mosul.
- Hammu Al Kaddu: Built by the Kaddu family around 1881, it has been destroyed.
- Al Khatun: Built by Mariam Khatun, daughter of Muhammad Pasha al-Jalili in 1826, it held more than fifty-five rare manuscripts; these and the school have been destroyed.
- Khuzam: Attached to Khuzam Mosque in Old Mosul, it was built in 1696 and later renovated by Shaykh al-Islam Abu Huda Al-Sayyad by order of the Ottoman Sultan himself. It was of great value to the Old City for containing most of the rarest manuscripts on Mosul history, which were destroyed during the battle for Mosul.

The above list initially contained more than forty-six schools and thirty-three private libraries. However, the author preferred to select a few examples of the schools to illustrate the destruction of the cultural space in Mosul during the battle against ISIS.

Conclusion

As an historian who has not only documented the destruction of Mosul's cultural heritage but also witnessed some of it first-hand, and who is now following closely the reconstruction and preservation of this heritage, I tend to be pessimistic about the future of Mosul and its culture. We have seen how a lack of understanding of Mosul's cultural heritage may cause conflicts and damage memory. One of this author's key observations is that the international response to the destruction of cultural heritage in Mosul has been inadequate. It is evident that international organizations and foreign states have different interests and view the city's heritage from diverse perspectives. The US Department of State and the governments of France and other nations perceive the community as divided and in conflict, rather than recognizing that the city has just experienced the largest known destruction of heritage in history. This view has created several problems and triggered conflicts over narratives of whose heritage deserves priority. It began with the preservation of ancient heritage, particularly the Assyrian historical sites. The argument made by both scholars and international organizations was that Iraq's ancient history mattered more than its recent past. However, this argument over what is important and what is not reflects the legacy of colonialism. Ancient history has been a part of colonialism ever since the foreign projects for archaeological excavation began, and Mosul's history ceased to be an element of visual memory. Its ancient legacy is more closely connected to the great international museums than to the place where it originally existed.

This divisive and invidious perspective is triggering more conflicts and is harming the people's visual memory. The concept of the 'People of Mosul' or 'Mosulis', in the current discourse, is being used not to refer to the city as a whole; rather, it is limited to the Sunni Muslim community. When Mosul's cultural heritage was destroyed, a public space, where people developed their narrative, also vanished. Heritage was replaced by rubble and the space with divisive discourse.

The visual memory of Mosul was subject to two factors; one was the need to preserve the past by protecting its legacy after 2003, when the US invaded Iraq and changed the balance of power in the country. The second occurred when ISIS destroyed the heritage of Nineveh. It was, in many cases, a response to the accusation from the other communities that the Muslim community of Mosul did not make sufficient efforts to protect its heritage.

Therefore, one of the consequences of ISIS's destruction of the heritage was the modification of time and space. The question is not just whose heritage it is, but what the umbrella of this heritage should be? Moreover, what historical period should be prioritized in the historical narrative? When ISIS occupied Mosul, it carried out the systematic destruction of the city's identity. First, it forced the city's non-Muslim inhabitants to flee, destroying their heritage in order to remove them from the city's history. Then came the destruction of ancient Assyrian and cultural sites. After this brutality against Mosul's non-Islamic history, ISIS shifted to the Muslim community, where it began to systematically destroy Islamic archaeological sites, as well as museums, libraries and manuscripts.

ISIS aimed to impose its narrative of history on Mosul, to cause a change in its social system, after targeting its multi-ethnic and multi-religious society. The consequences of ISIS's occupation are beyond imagining. To re-establish, revitalize and stabilize the city will require years. ISIS's occupation also led to the emergence of an intellectual discourse in Mosul that brought back the question of the city's historical and geopolitical position within Iraq and the wider region, as well as the impact of the First World War on the city and its population.

Finally, I argue that any effort to preserve Mosul's cultural heritage cannot succeed, or will trigger more conflicts and do more damage, if it does not take into account the micro-details of the formation of that heritage by protecting the Old City of Mosul while rebuilding it.

Appendix: Maps and list of destroyed Islamic historical sites in Old Mosul

Figure 4.4: Destroyed Islamic historical sites in Old Mosul: An Assessment.

Note: Numbers refers to the historical sites in Table 1 below.

Source: MIBACT 2017.

Table 4.1: List of destroyed Islamic historical sites in Old Mosul

# on the map	Property name	District	Lat	Long	Property type
1	Abariqi, Mosque of al- [and/or Mosque of al-Ridwani ?]	Mosul	36,334586	43,130687	Mosque
2	Abbas, Mosque of al-	Mosul	36,342635	43,132902	Mosque
3	Abu al-'Ala', Mosque of	Mosul	36,341282	43,131585	Mosque
4	Aghawat Mosque, al-	Mosul	36,344651	43,136588	Mosque
5	'Ajil al-Yawur, Mosque of	Mosul	36,325565	43,139025	Mosque
6	Ali al-Asghar (Ibn al-Hanafiyya), Shrine of	Mosul	36,343508	43,126205	Shrine
7	al-Tahira Church and Syriac Catholic Diocese	Mosul	36,344633	43,132378	Church
8	al-Tahira, Syriac Orthodox Church	Mosul	36,344066	43,132252	Church
9	Armenian Church	Mosul	36,344521	43,132126	Church
10	Bab al Seray	Mosul	36,342446	43,134893	Public building
11	Bash Tabiya Castle	Mosul	36,355166	43,121514	Archaeol. site
12	Basha/Pasha Mosque, al-	Mosul	36,343122	43,135893	Mosque
14	Dausat Ali, Shrine of	Mosul	36,343001	43,124714	Shrine
15	Hajj Zuheir, Bayt	Mosul	36,340023	43,132369	Historic house
16	Hammam of the Castle	Mosul	36,346015	43,134519	Archaeol. site
17	Hamo al-Qado Mosque	Mosul	36,345005	43,134519	Mosque
18	Historic Church	Mosul	36,34443	43,132484	Church
20	Jidadiya as-Sharqiyah, al-	Mosul	36,339218	43,139235	Public building
21	Imam Abdul al-Rahman, Shrine of al-	Mosul	36,349894	43,124601	Shrine
22	Imam al Bahir, Mosque and Shrine of al-	Mosul	36,344306	43,12049	Mosque and shrine
23	Imam 'Ali al-Hadi, Shrine of al-	Mosul	36,337462	43,120509	Shrine
24	Imam 'Awn al-Din, Shrine of al- (known as Ibn al-Hasan)	Mosul	36,339077	43,131052	Shrine

25	Imam Ibrahim, Mosque of al-	Mosul	36,345607	43,129755	Mosque
26	Imam Muhsin, Mosque of al-	Mosul	36,353046	43,122263	Mosque and shrine
27	Imam Yahya ibn al-Qasim, Mashhad al-	Mosul	36,35456	43,122788	Shrine
28	Imam Zayd ibn ʿAli, Shrine of al-	Mosul	36,33557	43,126825	Shrine
29	Isa Dadah, Shrine of	Mosul	36,350199	43,127919	Shrine
30	Jamsheet Mosque	Mosul	36,34485	43,126759	Mosque
31	Juwaighati, Mosque	Mosul	36,336102	43,129535	Mosque
32	Kara Quinn, Islamic Cemetery	Tell Kayf	36,400478	43,045355	Cemetery
33	Khatun, Mosque of Maryam al-	Mosul	36,343817	43,133859	Mosque
34	Khazam Mosque, al-	Mosul	36,339993	43,133226	Mosque
35	Khazraj Mosque, al-	Mosul	36,339916	43,123789	Mosque
36	Kherbet Al-Giamusiyya (AASI map 131, no 56)	Mosul	36,393699	43,075081	Archaeol. site
37	Khidr, Mosque of al- or al-Jamiʿ al-Ahmar, al-Jamiʿ al-Mujahidi	Mosul	36,339998	43,140331	Mosque
38	Latin Church, Monastery of the Dominican Fathers and Convent of Katrina Siena Nuns	Mosul	36,340674	43,12718	Church, monastery and convent
39	Madrasa al Babyl	Mosul	36,339023	43,126939	Madrasa
40	Mahkama Mosque, al-	Mosul	36,339512	43,132816	Mosque
41	Mahmudin/Hamudin, Mosque of al-	Mosul	36,338411	43,12234	Mosque
42	Makkawi, Mosque, al-	Mosul	36,345904	43,127541	Mosque
43	Mar Abdul Ahad, School	Mosul	36,340006	43,12861	Public building
44	Mar Ahudeni/Ahudemmah, Syrian Orthodox Church	Mosul	36,336118	43,127997	Church
45	Mar Ishaya, Church of	Mosul	36,34864	43,129117	Church

(*continued on next page*)

Table 4.1: Continued

# on the map	Property name	District	Lat	Long	Property type
46	Mar Jirjis, Church of	Mosul	36,340416	43,125107	Church
47	Mar Pythion Church	Mosul	36,338256	43,128386	Church
48	Mar Thoma, Syriac Catholic Church of	Mosul	36,341168	43,125154	Church
49	Mar Thoma, Syriac Orthodox Church of	Mosul	36,34077	43,125322	Church
50	Maskinta Church	Mosul	36,338472	43,125522	Church
51	Mosque and Husayniyya (Rawdat al-Wadi?)	Hamdaniya	36,349216	43,14716	Mosque
52	Mosul Central Library	Hamdaniya	36,34602	43,151895	Public building
53	Mosul Museum	Mosul	36,337773	43,139372	Public building
54	Musaffi Mosque, al-	Mosul	36,346414	43,132228	Mosque
55	Nabi Daniyal Shrine	Mosul	36,344736	43,123654	Shrine
56	Nabi Jirjis, Mosque of al-	Mosul	36,344363	43,130227	Mosque
57	Nabi Sheeth, Mosque and Shrine of al-	Mosul	36,334581	43,135187	Mosque and shrine
60	Niqab, Mosque of al-	Mosul	36,353279	43,121766	Mosque
61	Nu'maniya Mosque, al-	Mosul	36,341128	43,130357	Mosque
62	Nur al Din Minaret/al Habda	Mosul	36,343482	43,126406	Minaret
63	Nur al-Din, Mosque of	Mosul	36,342786	43,126738	Mosque
64	Omar al-Aswad, Mosque of	Mosul	36,337975	43,12863	Mosque
65	Police Station	Mosul	36,341901	43,135257	Public building
66	Qabr al-Bint, also known as Ali Ibn al-Athir, Tomb of	Mosul	36,341268	43,116513	Shrine
67	Qadhib al-Ban al-Mawsili, Mosque and Mausoleum of	Mosul	36,339829	43,115313	Mosque and shrine
69	Rabiya, Mosque of al-	Mosul	36,339508	43,128543	Mosque

70	Sabunji Mosque, al-	Mosul	36,340621	43,138396	Mosque
71	Saffar Mosque	Mosul	36,341157	43,127031	Mosque
72	Sarj Mosque, al-	Mosul	36,33895	43,138264	Mosque
73	Shah Zanan (or Umm al-Tisʿa), Shrine of	Mosul	36,342467	43,124708	Shrine
74	Shaikh Rashid Lolan, Tomb	Hamdaniya	36,348323	43,159245	Shrine
75	Sharif Khan (Tarbisu), Palace	Tell Kayf	36,408644	43,077193	Palace compound
76	Shaykh ʿAbdal, Madrasa of al-	Mosul	36,343137	43,134608	Madrasa
77	Shaykh Abdal, Mosque of al-	Mosul	36,342936	43,134481	Mosque
78	Shaykh al-Shatt, Shrine of	Mosul	36,349064	43,130949	Shrine
79	Shaykh Fathi, Mosque and Tomb/Shrine of al-	Mosul	36,346839	43,117765	Mosque and shrine
80	Shaykh Fathi, Mosque and Tomb/Shrine of al-	Mosul	36,346443	43,117591	Mosque and shrine
81	Shaykh Fathi, Mosque and Tomb/Shrine of al-	Mosul	36,346841	43,118062	Mosque and shrine
82	Sheik al-Shatt, Mosque of	Mosul	36,349104	43,131059	Mosque
83	Shimoun al Safa Church and cemetery	Mosul	36,33789	43,12596	Church and cemetery
84	Shrine (of al-Imamayn Hamid wa Mahmud?) adjoining to the Mosque of al-Mahmudin/al-Hamidin	Mosul	36,338414	43,122224	Shrine
85	Sitt Nafisa, Mosque and Shrine of al- (Hammam al-Saray Mosque, tomb of al-Shaykh Yunus, and Shrine of al-Sitt Nafisa)	Mosul	36,342715	43,128614	Mosque and shrine
86	Suleyman Sayeg, Bayt	Mosul	36,344994	43,132904	Historic house
87	Sultan Uways, Mosque and Shrine of al-	Mosul	36,345418	43,123369	Mosque and shrine

(*continued on next page*)

Table 4.1: Continued

# on the map	Property name	District	Lat	Long	Property type
88	Tahira Church and Chaldean Archdiocese	Mosul	36,353232	43,123207	Church
89	Tahira Syriac Orthodox Church, al- (al Tahr al-Fawqaniyya)	Mosul	36,352864	43,120321	Church
90	Tikritains/al-Bayt al-Tikriti, Mosque	Mosul	36,336029	43,128173	Mosque
91	Tutanchi, Bayt al-	Mosul	36,341535	43,130792	Historic house
92	Um al-Ma'ona Church	Mosul	36,334116	43,138618	Church
93	Umariya/ Omariya Mosque, al-	Mosul	36,33506	43,130899	Mosque
94	Unidentified Mosque	Mosul	36,351618	43,12681	Mosque
95	Unknown Mosque (Bakr el-Afandi?)	Mosul	36,342598	43,136626	Mosque
96	Unknown structure	Mosul	36,347085	43,131234	

Note: the list was combined with information collected by the author and matched with the survey created by the Italian Ministry of Culture (MIBACT 2017) and other sources including but not limited to interviews, dataset, personal documentation and archival recourses.

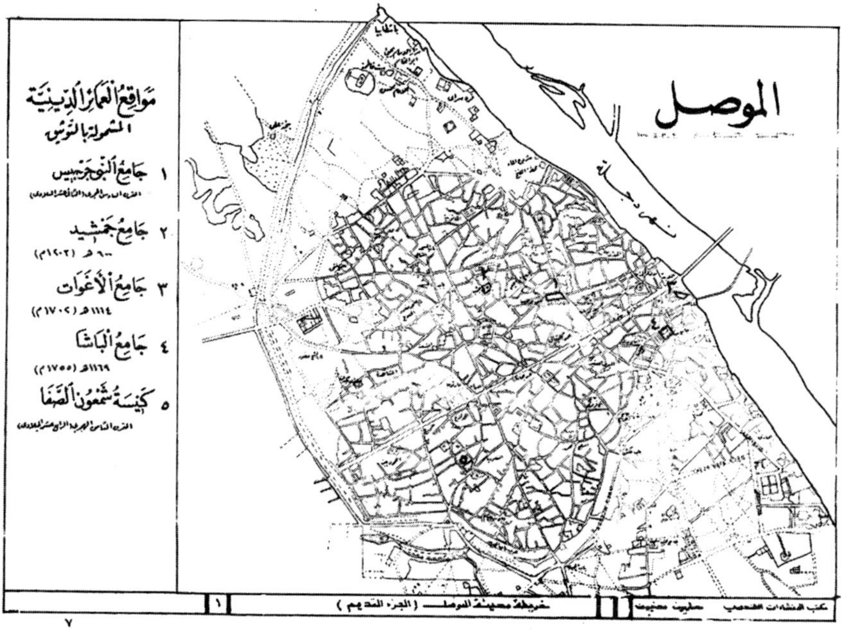

Figure 4.5: Map of the main historical mosques in Old Mosul.

Source: Dhannun 1983.

Figure 4.6: Jamshid Mosque.

Source: Dhannun 1983.

Figure 4.7: Ruins of Al-Nuri Mosque, 2018.

Figure 4.8: Hadbaa Minaret, 2013.

Figure 4.9: Suq Al-Haddadin, 2019.
Source: Mosul Eye.

Figure 4.10: Destruction of the Old Markets in Old Mosul, 2018.
Source: Saad Hadi.

Figure 4.11: Khan and old markets, Old Mosul, 2018.
Source: Saad Hadi.

Figure 4.12: Ruins of Sawwafa market, 2018.
Source: Mosul Eye.

Figure 4.13: Ruins of Khuzam Mosque, 2019.
Source: Mosul Eye.

Figure 4.14: Parts of Bab-l Saray Suq under reconstruction, 2018.
Source: Mosul Eye.

Figure 4.15: Suq Al Haddadin, 2019.
Source: Ali Al Baroodi.

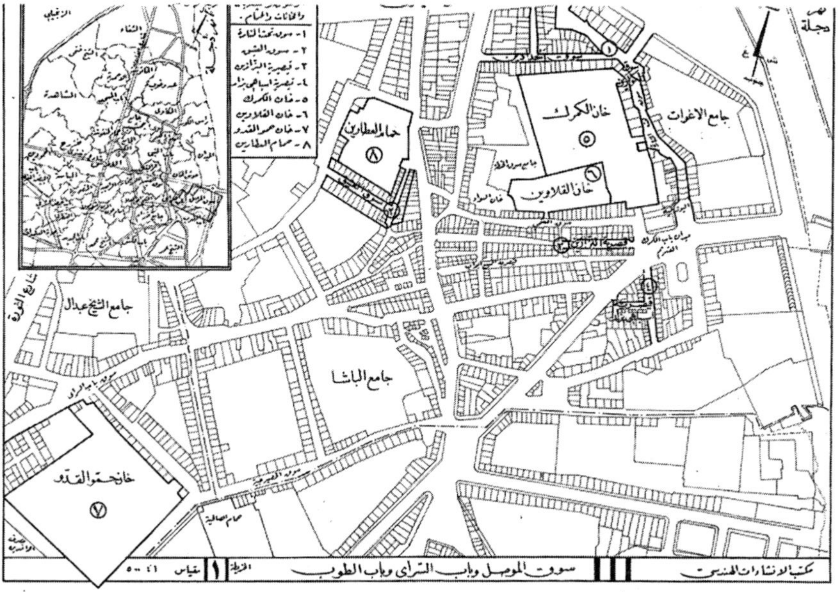

Figure 4.16: Map of the Suqs of Old Mosul.
Source: Dhannun 1983.

Note on the sources used in the chapter

The author relied for his primary sources on data that he collected when he was living under ISIS rule in 2014–15, as well as on documents in his possession including: (a) private collection of documents published by ISIS in Mosul; (b) list of the destroyed historical sites of Mosul, collected by the author; (c) list of the destroyed Islamic *kuttabs* and madrasas of Mosul; (d) list of the destroyed statues and monuments of Mosul; (e) the author's unpublished manuscript (Mohammed 2019). Some data cited in this chapter can also be found at Mosul Eye website, where the author collected and published data on Mosul's reconstruction. The author conducted some interviews (using Skype, Facetime, WhatsApp and phone calls) with: (a) Saud Al-Jalili, the great-grandson of Husain Pasha Al-Jalili, Mosul, 2019. Saud Al Jalili is a judge working in the general court of Mosul. He is known for holding the archives of the Jalili family and is responsible for managing their properties in Old Mosul. He was also the director of the renovation of Al-Pasha Mosque; (b) Professor Amir Al-Jumaily, head of the Mosul School of

Archaeology, Mosul University, 2017, 2018, 2019; (c) several people from Mosul including students, activists and governmental officials, 2019. Other sources were confidential records of meetings between the author and several historians and archaeologists in Mosul during the ISIS occupation. The meetings were held inside the house of a Mosuli archaeologist and discussed the situation of Mosul, its history and its heritage. The quotations from these records were included in the text without reference for the protection of the participants.

References

Abū Shāmah, ʻAbd al-Raḥmān ibn Ismāʻīl (1956), *Kitāb al-rawḍatayn fī akhbār al-dawlatayn al-Nūrīyah wa-al-Ṣalāḥīyah* (On the News of the Nuria and Salahiyah States), Cairo, Lajnat al-Ta'lif wa-al-Tarjimah wa-al-Nashr

Al-Ali Beg, Manhal Ismail (2005), *Tarikh al khadamat al waqfiyya fi al-Mawṣil, 1249-1337H/1834-1918M* (History of endowment services in Mosul, 1249–1337 AH/1834-1918 AD), Thesis, Mosul University

Al-Aqeedi, Rasha (2017), 'Mosul Mourns Its Minaret, Sort Of', in *The American Interest*, 12 July, https://wp.me/p4ja0Z-FXY

Al-Hayali, Akram Mohammed Yahya Jassim (2017), *Khutat Madinat al Mawsil Khilal 'Al 'Asr 'al 'Uthmani min khilal 'al Mabani 'al Shakhisa* (Mosul District During the Ottoman Period According to the Architecture Ruins, 1516–1918), Riga, Noor Publishing

Borges,Jorge Luis (2004), *The Aleph and Other Stories*, London, Penguin

Chalabī, Dāwūd (1927), *Kitāb makhṭūṭāt al-Mawṣil* (Manuscripts of Mosul), Baghdad, Maṭbaʻat al-Furāt, http://hdl.handle.net/2333.1/bg79cr0q

Al-Dabbagh, Abdulkhaliq Khalil (1956), *Muʻjam amthāl al-Mawṣil al-ʻāmmīyah. Sharḥ wa-taḥlīl* (Dictionary of vernacular proverbs of Mosul. Explanation and analysis), 2 vol., Mosul, Al Hadaf, http://hdl.handle.net/2333.1/pzgmsdpt

Dhannun, Yusuf (1983), *Al'-Ama'ir al-Diniyyah fi Madinat al-Mousul* (The Architecture of the Religious Buildings of Mosul), Mosul, State Organization of Antiquities & Heritage

Daniel, E. Valentine (1996), *Charred Lullabies. Chapters in an Anthropography of Violence*, Princeton, Princeton University Press

Dewachi, Said (1963), *Jawami' al Mawsil fi Mukhtalaf al 'Usur* (The mosques of Mosul through the ages), Baghdad, Matba'at Shafik

Elisséeff, Nikita (1995), 'Nur al-Din Mahmud b. Zanki', inBosworth, C. Edmund et al. (eds), *The Encyclopaedia of Islam, Vol. VIII: Ned-Sam*, Leiden, Brill, p. 127–133, https://scholar.harvard.edu/files/martinkramer/files/ei2.pdf

Ibn al-Athīr, 'Izz al-Dīn (2008), *The Chronicle of Ibn al-Athīr for the Crusading Period from al-Kamil fi'l-Ta'rikh. Pt 2: The Years 541-589/1146-1193. The Age of Nur al-Din and Saladin*, translated by Donald Sidney Richards, Aldershot/ Burlington, Ashgate

Janabi, Hashim Khudayyr (1982), *al-Tarkīb al-dākhilī lī-madīnat al-Mawṣil al-qadīmah. Dirāsah fī-jughrāfīyat al-mudun* (The Urban Structure of Old Mosul. A Study in the Geography of Cities), Mosul, University of Mosul

Jum'a, Ahmed Qasim (1989) *Al Ta'thirat al mi'mariyya bayna Misr wa al 'Iraq fi al 'Asr al 'Islami* (Architectural influences between Egypt and Iraq during the Islamic ages), Mosul, Al hay'a al 'amma liqusur al thaqafa

Kātib al-Isfahānī, 'Imād al-Dīn Muḥammad ibn Muḥammad (1987), *al-Barq al-Shāmī. al-Juz' al-khāmis* (The Syrian lightning. Part V), edited by Faleh Husseyn, Amman, Mu'assasat 'Abd al-Ḥamīd Shūmān

Kemp, Percy (1979), *Mosul and Mosuli Historians of the Jalīlī Era, 1726–1834*, PhD Thesis, University of Oxford

Khoury, Dina Rizk (1997), *State and Provincial Society in the Ottoman Empire. Mosul, 1540–1834*, Cambridge/New York, Cambridge University Press

MIBACT-Italian Ministry of Cultural Heritage and Activities and Tourism (2017), *A Systematic Assessment of Daesh-Inflicted Damages on Iraqi Heritage Repertories and Satellite Enquiry on Mosul City and Other Archaeological Sites*

Mohammed, Omar (2016), *Istikhlaf: Muslim Brotherhood version of the Caliphate*, Mosul, unpublished

Mohammed, Omar (2017), 'Mosul and Its Remains: Al-Nuri Grand Mosque, History, Identity', in *Oriental Studies*, 8 October, https://wp.me/p1ArJc-Kc

Mohammed, Omar (2018), 'Eye of the Storm: The Historian Known as Mosul Eye on Documenting What ISIS Were Trying to Destroy', in *Index on Censorship*, Vol. 47, No. 1 (April), p. 47–49, https://doi.org/10.1177/0306422018770114

Mohammed, Omar (2019), *The New History of Al-Nuri Mosque and its Minaret. The Story of Their Destruction*, unpublished

Muhammad, Munqidh Sadiq (2011), *Tarikh al khadamat al waqfiyya fi al-Mawṣil, 1249-1337H/1834-1918M* (History of endowment services in Mosul, 1249–1337 AH/1834-1918 AD), Thesis, Babylon University

Patton, Douglas (1991), *Badr Al-Din Lu'lu'. Atabeg of Mosul, 1211–1259*, Seattle, University of Washington Press

Qaddawi, Alaa Mahmud (2012), *Tārīkh al-'Irāq fī 'ahday al-Qarah Qūyunlū wa-al-Āq Qūyunlū, 814-914H/1411-1508M* (History of Iraq during the Qara Qoyunlu and Aq Qoyunlu periods, 814–914 AH/1411-1508 AD), Amman, Dār Ghaydā' lil-Nashr wa-al-Tawzī

Qaddawi, Alaa Mahmud (2015), *al-Mūṣil wa-al-Jazīrah al-Furātīyah fī 'ahd dawlat al-Maghūl al-Aylakhānīyah, 656-735H, 1258-1335M. Dirāsah taḥlīlīyah 'an al-iḥtilāl wa-al-muqāwmah wa-al-jawānib al-ḥaḍārīyah* (Mosul and the Euphrates Island during the era of the Ilkhanid Mongol state, 656–735 AH, 1258–1335 AD. An analytical study of occupation, resistance, and civilizational aspects), Amman, Dār Ghaydā' lil-Nashr wa-al-Tawzī

Raby, Julian (2004), 'Nur Al-Din, the Qastal al-Shuaybiyya, and the "Classical Revival"', in *Muqarnas*, Vol. 21, p. 289–310

Said, Edward (1977), *Orientalism*, London, Penguin Books

Socin, A. (1847), 'Der arabische Dialekt von Mosul und Märdin' in *Zeitschrift der Deutschen Morgenländischen Gesellschaft*, Vol. 1, http://menadoc.bibliothek.uni-halle.de/dmg/periodical/titleinfo/48123

Tabbaa, Yasser (1982), *The Architectural Patronage of Nur al-Din, 1146–1174*, PhD thesis, New York University

'Umarī, Yāsīn ibn Khayr Allāh al-Khaṭīb (1955), *Munyat al-udabā' fī tārīkh al-Mūṣil al-ḥadbā'* (The Biographical Dictionary of the Writers of Mosul), edited by Said al-Dewachi, Mosul, Maṭba'at al-Hadaf

'Umarī, Yāsīn ibn Khayr Allāh al-Khaṭīb (1974), *Zubdat al-Āthār al-jalīyah fī al-ḥawādith al-arḍīyah* (Selected Events from the History of Mosul), edited by Dāwūd Chalabī, Najaf, Maṭba'at al-Ādāb

Urry, John (1995), 'How Societies Remember the Past', in *The Sociological Review*, Vol. 43, No. 1 suppl., p. 45–65

Yahya, Akram M. (2012), 'Khutat Khanat Madiynat 'alMawsil fi 'al'Ahd al 'Uthmani' (Plans of Mosul Khans in the Ottoman Period), in *Mosoliya Studies*, Vol. 8, No. 38, p. 25–62, https://moss.mosuljournals.com/article_61419.html

al-Zarkali, Khair al-Din (2007), *al-A'lām. Qāmūs tarājim li-ashhar al-rijāl wa-al-nisā' min al-'Arab wa-al-musta'ribīn wa-al-mustashriqīn* (The Biographical Dictionary of the Notable Men and Women: Arabs, Arabists and Orientalists), 17th ed., Beirut, Dār al-'Ilm lil-Malāyīn, 2007, Vol. 5

Abdul Salam Taha

Chapter 5: The Role of Academia in Enabling the Illicit Antiquities Market: The Damage to Iraq's Cultural Heritage

Scholars from all over the world are engaged in debates over the study and publication of unprovenanced artefacts and the loss of knowledge that results when the archaeological context of artefacts is unknown.[1] Academics from various disciplines regularly come into contact during the course of their research with traded cultural objects that are unprovenanced. Even if such artefacts carry historical information that is to some degree independent of their provenance, the extent of this information outside the object's archaeological context is limited. Experts who follow the flow of objects on the antiquities market are concerned not only with context and provenance but also with broader issues such as ownership history and the impact that the academic study of unprovenanced artefacts has on the antiquities market.

The aim of this chapter is to draw attention to the involvement of academic experts with the antiquities trade. It uses a series of case studies to illustrate how academic studies facilitate and enable the acquisition of antiquities with no provenance history, support illicit antiquity market actors and increase the price value of such antiquities. The main focus here is to examine the forms of involvement of academics who study ancient artefacts and explore how, through their research, they associate with antiquities collectors and dealers, thereby helping the trade, albeit indirectly. To investigate the parameters of this facilitation, five case studies are presented, each one clarifying some aspects of academic involvement with the antiquities trade.

The case studies detailed in this chapter are restricted to the consideration of unprovenanced objects that have been proven to have been or are suspected by the courts of having been looted or stolen from archaeological sites or storage vaults. An 'academic expert' is defined as an academically qualified individual

1 Perhaps we should distinguish between two terms: 'provenance', which defines the ownership history of an artefact inclusive of its known archaeological find-spot, and 'provenience', which covers the find-spot only (Brodie and Kersel 2014: 200).

who works on specific items outside museums. For convenience, these objects will be referred to as 'antiquities'. The studies discussed were conducted by academics who work in the field of archaeology, and in related disciplines such as epigraphy and art history.

5.1 The Narām-Sîn Fragment

In May 2003, the Metropolitan Museum of Art in New York organized an exhibition called 'Art of the First Cities: The Third Millennium B.C. from the Mediterranean to the Indus' (Aruz and Wallenfels 2003). Among the pieces exhibited was a triangular piece of limestone,[2] 11 cm in height and 13.5 cm wide, depicting Narām-Sîn, one of the famous rulers of the Akkadian Empire (Figure 5.1). According to the literature that was provided in the exhibition, this piece was lent by Jonathan Rosen, an American entrepreneur based in New York who owns one of the world's largest private collections of Mesopotamian antiquities.[3]

Professor Donald P. Hansen, a renowned archaeologist in Near Eastern studies,[4] studied the object and wrote an academic article about it primarily intended for a small readership of experts (Hansen 2002). Hansen obviously had visited Rosen's collection before the exhibition to carry out his study, and it is logical to expect that his expert conclusions must have had an effect on the piece's standing monetary value. The issue of the fragment's origin was addressed in a footnote in his publication, where the object was described as being of 'unknown provenance',[5]

---

2 Collector/Owner: The Rosen Foundation (Jonathan and Jeannette Rosen), New York. Scholar/Institution: Donald P. Hansen/Institute of Fine Arts, New York.

3 Jonathan P. Rosen steers the Rosen Group, a privately held real estate development and management consortium specialized in shopping centres, office buildings and other commercial property. Rosen is a major collector of coins and ancient art and a generous donor to the Lands Museum Jerusalem via his foundation, recently giving the outfit a seven-figure gift. Other grantees have included the American Friends of Israel Museum and the Educational Institute Oholei Torah (source: https://www.rosengroupinc.co).

4 Donald P. Hansen (1931–2007), PhD in Near Eastern Studies, gained his initial professional training at the Oriental Institute of the University of Chicago. He joined the Institute of Fine Arts, New York in 1963, and participated in excavations all over southern Iraq, including in Nippur, and served as field director at Mendes, Tell Abu Salabikh and Al-Hiba. See Institute of Fine Arts (2007).

5 'The horned-crowned Narām-Sîn was portrayed as a deity alongside Ishtar. Four prisoners, in humiliating restraints, attested to the military prowess that made Narām-Sîn the dominant ruler of his day. The piece appeared to be one of the few of royal

while the Met publication referred to it as coming from 'Mesopotamia', a generic term that historically and geographically covers a vast area, including Iraq and parts of Syria, southern Turkey and also the Ahwaz region of Iran.

The issue of this object's provenance was broached in the following terms.

Scholary views

- Donald P. Hansen: 'some colleagues would not have written about the fragment [. . .] its imagery was so unusual that it merited a place in the scholarly literature. [. . .] It is a great piece of art historically, and I thought it should be known' (Gottlieb and Meier 2003a).
- Jane C. Waldbaum (President of the Archaeological Institute of America): 'If a reputable scholar publishes an article about an [unprovenanced] artefact, they're giving it the imprimatur of authenticity based on their scholarship and expertise' (Gottlieb and Meier 2003a).

It is worth remembering that in the 1970s, the Archaeological Institute of America forbade its members from making initial presentations about such artefacts in its journals and at its annual meeting. Since the Met exhibition in 2003, the Narām-Sîn Fragment has not been viewed again publicly.

5.2 The Garšana cuneiform tablets

In 2003, the Rosen Foundation donated a total of 1,679 cuneiform tablets[6] to the Department of Near Eastern Studies at Cornell University, in return for tax deductions. Cornell accepted the donation on assurances that the tablets had been legally acquired (Gottlieb and Meier 2003b). However, hardly any verifiable evidence of these objects' provenance was provided or cited in studies published on this collection. Regardless, David Owen of the University of Cornell was invited to assist.[7] He promptly organized a programme of research and publication for the collection (Owen 2007b).

Akkadian patronage to survive.' An object that has never been seen, or heard of. See Gottlieb and Meier (2003a). See also Hansen (2003: 206–7).

6 Collector/Owner: The Rosen Foundation, New York. Scholar/Institution: David I. Owen/Cornell University, New York.

7 David I. Owen, PhD in Mediterranean Studies from Brandeis University, 1969, is the Bernard and Jane Schapiro Emeritus Professor of Ancient Near Eastern and Judaic Studies and Curator of Tablet Collections in the Jonathan and Jeannette Rosen Ancient Near Eastern Studies Seminar and Tablet Conservation Laboratory. In addition to

extensive archaeological fieldwork in Turkey, Italy, Greece, Cyprus and Israel from 1961–88, Professor Owen taught courses in the Sumerian and the Akkadian languages, in Near Eastern and biblical history, and in archaeology. He is currently retired from teaching. See his profile on the Cornell University website: https://neareasternstudies.cornell.edu/david-i-owen.

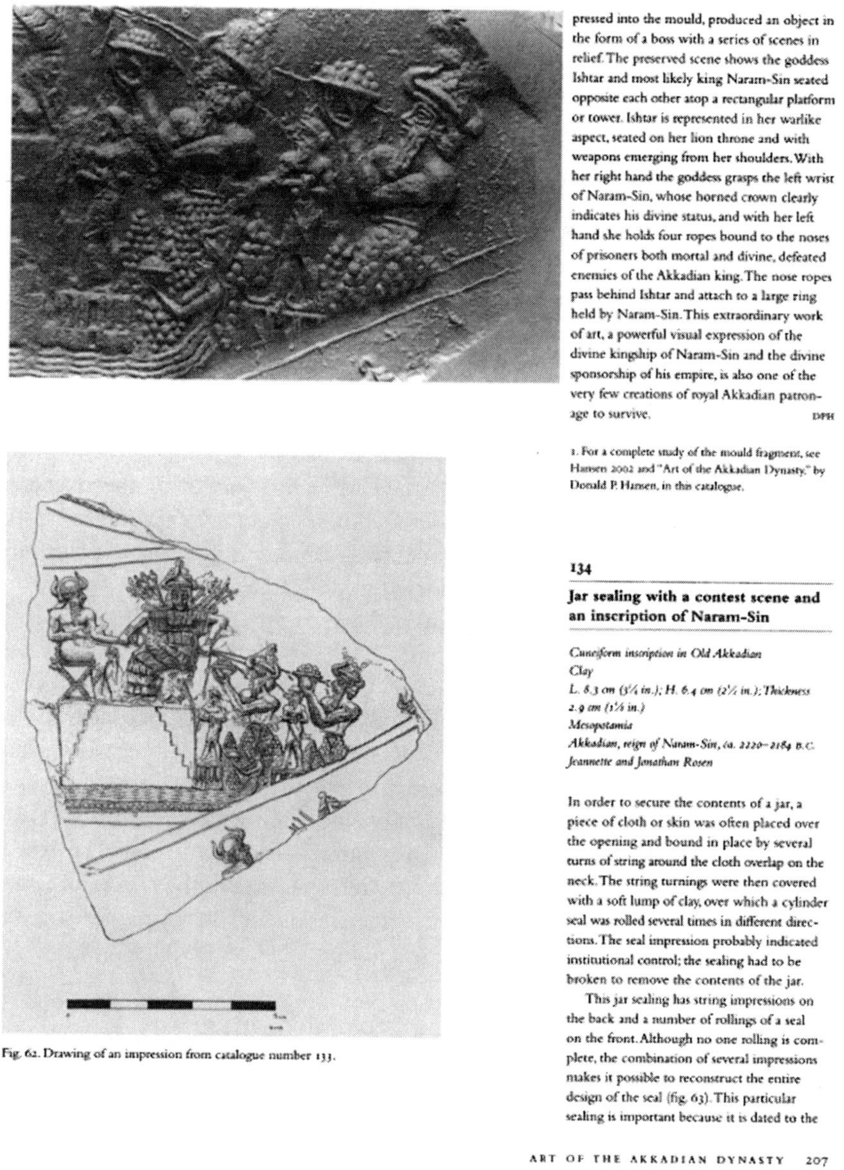
pressed into the mould, produced an object in the form of a boss with a series of scenes in relief. The preserved scene shows the goddess Ishtar and most likely king Naram-Sin seated opposite each other atop a rectangular platform or tower. Ishtar is represented in her warlike aspect, seated on her lion throne and with weapons emerging from her shoulders. With her right hand the goddess grasps the left wrist of Naram-Sin, whose horned crown clearly indicates his divine status, and with her left hand she holds four ropes bound to the noses of prisoners both mortal and divine, defeated enemies of the Akkadian king. The nose ropes pass behind Ishtar and attach to a large ring held by Naram-Sin. This extraordinary work of art, a powerful visual expression of the divine kingship of Naram-Sin and the divine sponsorship of his empire, is also one of the very few creations of royal Akkadian patronage to survive. DPH

1. For a complete study of the mould fragment, see Hansen 2002 and "Art of the Akkadian Dynasty," by Donald P. Hansen, in this catalogue.

Fig. 62. Drawing of an impression from catalogue number 133.

134

Jar sealing with a contest scene and an inscription of Naram-Sin

Cuneiform inscription in Old Akkadian
Clay
L. 8.3 cm (3¼ in.); H. 6.4 cm (2½ in.); Thickness 2.9 cm (1⅛ in.)
Mesopotamia
Akkadian, reign of Naram-Sin, ca. 2220–2184 B.C.
Jeannette and Jonathan Rosen

In order to secure the contents of a jar, a piece of cloth or skin was often placed over the opening and bound in place by several turns of string around the cloth overlap on the neck. The string turnings were then covered with a soft lump of clay, over which a cylinder seal was rolled several times in different directions. The seal impression probably indicated institutional control; the sealing had to be broken to remove the contents of the jar.

This jar sealing has string impressions on the back and a number of rollings of a seal on the front. Although no one rolling is complete, the combination of several impressions makes it possible to reconstruct the entire design of the seal (fig. 63). This particular sealing is important because it is dated to the

ART OF THE AKKADIAN DYNASTY 207

Figure 5.1: The Narām-Sîn Fragment.
Source: Hansen (2003: 206–7).

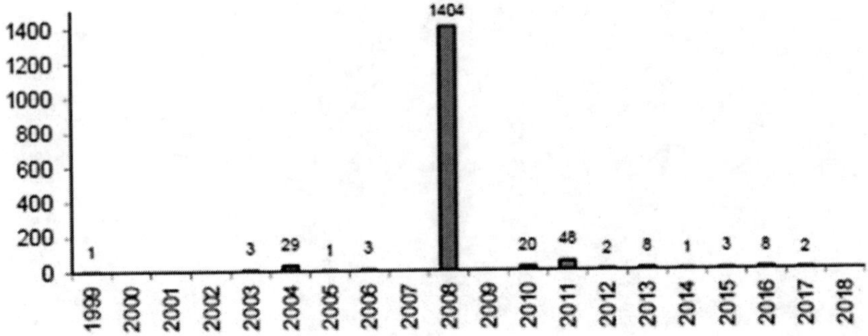

Figure 5.2: Cataloguing and publication of texts from Garšana.
Source: Molina (2019: 4).

Garšana was a royal town located in the Umma province of southern Iraq. Its precise location remains unknown. Looters found an archive that attested to the activities of the household of princess Simat-Ištaran and her husband Šu-Kabt, in the town itself, or somewhere in its surrounding area.

The first tablet publicly known from Garšana was auctioned on eBay in November 1999. Between this date and 2007, when the standard edition of Garšana texts by David Owen and Rudolf Mayr was published, only thirty-five texts from this site were published. The publication by Owen and Mayr (2007) presented 1,401 new texts from Garšana, 1,390 of which were kept at Cornell University, while the remaining eleven texts belonged to private collections. Since the publication of this study, ninety-seven more tablets from Garšana, kept in various collections, most of them again at Cornell University, have been catalogued or published. Figure 5.2 shows the evolution of the cataloguing and publication of Garšana texts to the present. The picture that emerges suggests that the looting of the site was carried out not long before 1999.[8]

Collecting antiquities versus financial advantages

Up until formal investigations were conducted, no information was published on the source of this collection, nor was anything said about the total cost of the purchase. Similarly, nothing was mentioned by the donor or the receiver about valuations done on the tablets for the purpose of estimating tax deductions.

8 Rosen has always maintained the claim that they were acquired by 1997 (Owen 2007b).

Later on, investigations revealed that the tablets were acquired in 1997 for 50,000 US dollars; and in 2003, Rosen declared them as a donation valued at a total of 950,000 US dollars, thereby benefiting from 900,000 US dollars in tax deductions (see Table 5.1). These figures clearly establish the monetary worth of this collection prior to the donation, which is obviously due to the scholar's intervention, well before the publication of the study in 2007.

The striking facts of this case are that the tablets had already been studied before the formal donation was arranged, and the analysis of their content was under way before they were donated to Cornell in 2003. Owen himself states that he started working on the Garšana tablets in 1997 (Owen 2007a: vii). The question is then whether the study of these objects prior to the donation resulted in a positive financial impact.

Scholarly views

In defence of the Garšana study programme, Owen declared that he believes 'scholars have a responsibility to preserve and publish such records of the past that are available, whether or not they have solid proof of provenance'. He additionally noted that there is not the least bit of evidence that proves that any scholar's involvement in the study and publication of unprovenanced artefacts encourages the looting of sites or affects the value of the antiquities in private collections (Owen 2007b: v–vi).

Suppression of provenance

This case raises serious questions regarding the suppression of provenance. Private collectors who purchase unprovenanced material may not give enough attention to due diligence before buying culturally sensitive material, but the act of acquiring them does give them access to at least part of the provenance history of these objects. Academics who work closely with collectors are also well placed to access such knowledge. Unfortunately, this information is rarely shared. In the case of the Garšana tablets, only minimal information was presented and it has done nothing to clarify this collection's provenance (Brodie 2011a: 419). Ultimately, it seems, a scholar like Owen is unwilling to upset the cartel of collectors that provide him with material for his research projects. Irrespective of the absence of information on provenance tracking, in Figure 5.3 the distribution of tablets from Garšana sites is illustrated in an informative chart.

A positive development for Iraq's recovery of its cultural property came recently in the form of a New York court of law ordering the return of 10,000

~~O F F I C I A L U S E O N L Y~~

DEPARTMENT OF HOMELAND SECURITY ICE R E P O R T O F I N V E S T I G A T I O N C O N T I N U A T I O N	PAGE 2 CASE NUMBER [redacted] REPORT NUMBER: 010

DETAILS OF INVESTIGATION

The SAC/New York, Office of Investigations has been conducting this investigation on [redacted] et al for importing art & antiquities from Iran and Iraq in violation of the Presidential Orders imposing sanctions with the aforementioned countries.

Other alleged violations of law include:

* The improper donation of Iraqi Cuneiform Tablets to Cornell University where [redacted] received a $900,000 tax deduction. [redacted] was the importer of record for 1,679. The total entered value for the Tablets were no more than $50,000.
* Trading with the Enemy Act by wire transferring money to third party accounts in Switzerland knowing that the funds would be further transmitted to accounts in Iran and Iraq.
* Falsely declaring the true country of origin of the Cuneiform Tablets and the Cylinder Seals on entry documents in order to introduce the items for sale in the US.

The investigation to date has not brought forth the appropriate information and evidence to substantiate the allegations in all of the above.

There is no dispute that the objects of art being the Cuneiform Tablets and the Cylinder Seals existed in what today's geography identifies as Iran and Iraq. What is not proven is when the objects of art were unearthed, excavated, looted, and when they were removed from their original site. Thus leaving the probability that the objects were removed prior to Cultural Property laws and the advent of the UNESCO Convention that took place in 1970. In that case, there is no violation of law without that information.

After a careful review and analysis of [redacted] banking information, there was no evidence that his payments were sent directly to accounts owned or controlled by Iran and/or Iraqi entities/persons. In addition, this office requested financial records of a non-US citizen, [redacted] who resides in London, via an MLAT to the Swiss Government. The responsive information only reflected [redacted] transactions and did not contain information relating to financial dealings by [redacted] Since [redacted] is not a US Citizen, we have no jurisdiction over his activities.

The issue regarding the tax deduction for the donation of the Cuneiform Tablets to Cornell University will be referred to the IRS by the Eastern District of New York.

~~O F F I C I A L U S E O N L Y~~

~~THIS DOCUMENT IS LOANED TO YOU FOR OFFICIAL USE ONLY AND REMAINS THE PROPERTY OF THE DEPARTMENT OF HOMELAND SECURITY, ICE. ANY FURTHER REQUEST FOR DISCLOSURE OF THIS DOCUMENT OR INFORMATION CONTAINED HEREIN SHOULD BE REFERRED TO ICE HEADQUARTERS TOGETHER WITH A COPY OF THE DOCUMENT.~~

ICE.2012FOIA10452.000011

Figure 5.3: Copy of investigation report by Homeland Security on Rosen's Garšana tablets.

Source: Molina (2019).

Table 5.1: Dispersion of texts from Garšana.

Australia	Anonimous private collection (Ballarat, VIC)	1
France	Private collection of Laurent Hebenstrei (Paris)	2
Germany	Private collection of P. Kress (Bochum)	3
Iran	National Museum of Iran (Tehran)	1
Iraq	Iraq Museum (Baghdad)	4
	Sulaimaniah Musaum (Sulaimaniah)	1
Israel	Av private collection (Jerusalem)	4
Italy	Banca d'Italia (Rome)	1
	Anonymous private collection (Rome)	1
Norway	Private collection of Martin Schøyen (Oslo)	22
Spain	Private collection (Barcelona)	
Spain	Private collection (Madrid)	2
USA	Cornell University (Ithaca, NY)	1,465
	Green Collection (Oklahoma City, OK)	4
	Private collection of E.S. (unlocated)	3
	Private collection of M. Cohen (unlocated)	2
	Private collection of P.J. (unlocated)	2
	Anonymous private collection (San Francisco, PA)	2
	Anonymous private collection (unlocated)	95
Unknow country	Anonymous private collections	8
Galleries, auction houses	Archaelogical Center (Tel Aviv-Jaffa, Israel)	1
	Drouout Montaigne (Paris, France)	1
	eBay (San José, CA, USA)	1
Total texts		**1,628**

Source: Molina (2019: 5).

cuneiform tablets from different sites in Iraq, in Cornell's possession, back to Iraq, their country of origin.

5.3 The Aramaic incantation bowls

University College London (UCL) decided in 1996 to conduct a special study via its Department of Hebrew and Jewish Studies, to research a total of 654 Aramaic incantation bowls[9] in collaboration with the Schøyen collection, a Norwegian

9 Collector/Owner: Martin Schøyen, Norway. Scholar/Institution: Shaul Shaked/Hebrew University of Jerusalem/ University College London.

group owned by Martin Schøyen who claimed ownership of the bowls. Professor Shaul Shaked of the Hebrew University of Jerusalem was appointed as leader of the research team (Shaked et al. 2013).[10] These ceramic flat-based bowls, which date from between AD 100 and 700, contain special inscriptions, mainly in Aramaic language, with a few in Syriac and Hebrew, and rarely in Arabic and Persian. Black ink was used to inscribe their inner surfaces, mostly spiralling outward from the centre. Generally speaking, they were intended to protect against evil forces. Such objects hold a wealth of information for understanding cults and religions at a specific time in history.

The records show that these bowls were first mentioned by the British excavator Austen Henry Layard, who referenced their archaeological context upon his discoveries in 1850 at Babylon and Nippur, but it's worth mentioning that the British Museum already owned two of them by 1841 (Layard 1853: 508–26). More extensive archaeological information related to the bowls was given in the study published by John Punnett Peters on the expedition to Nippur by the University of Pennsylvania (Peters 1897).

These bowls are usually to be found in the structural ruins of houses and were uncovered close to the surface. They are typically located under the floor in different corners of buildings, or even sometimes by door entrances, placed upside down. A typical house would usually contain one or more of them. To date, approximately 2,000 of those bowls are known, but only a few hundred have been studied and published. Most have been found in Iraq (Brodie 2008).

The chronical of the UCL study project goes back to early 1996, when Schøyen invited Professor Shaked to research his collection. To facilitate Shaked's efforts, Schøyen collaborated with the Department of Hebrew and Jewish Studies at UCL to host the collection. Accordingly, Shaked worked continuously on translating and publishing the Schøyen bowls without public knowledge until the mid-2000s. In September 2004, the Norwegian Broadcasting Corporation (NRK) produced a series of documentaries called 'The Manuscript Collector', a well-researched investigation into the activities of the Norwegian book and manuscript collector Martin Schøyen. The documentary revealed to a wide audience evidence of how the looting and destruction

10 Shaul Shaked, Professor Emeritus of Iranian Studies, Religious Studies, Aramaic and Magic in Late Antiquity. The Hebrew University, Jerusalem.

of archaeological heritage is ultimately financed by wealthy collectors and legitimized by naive scholars.

The hard-hitting investigation claimed that Schøyen's bowls were most likely looted from Iraq in 1992, in the aftermath of the 1991 Operation Desert Storm, when the United States and its allies pushed Iraq out of Kuwait. At that time, harsh international sanctions were imposed on Iraq, but the UN Security Council also passed a resolution related to the protection of Iraq's cultural heritage. Thus, the NRK documentary strongly suggests that Schøyen's acquisition of the bowls which has commenced from 1994 onwards was in violation of international resolutions.

On 14 February 2005, UCL commissioned an independent internal investigation to determine the provenance of Schøyen's collection of bowls. The report was delivered on 27 July 2006, but public access to it was restricted based on a settlement achieved with Schøyen in 2007, following his litigation against UCL for refusing to return the bowls to him. In 2009, the final findings of the UCL investigation were sent to the Library of the House of Lords by Lord Colin Renfrew, one of the committee members. In that same year, WikiLeaks made a copy of it available to the public. The report states clearly that in the early 1990s, Schøyen started buying bowls from different antiquity dealers in London. Most of the dealers involved in the trade with Schøyen's collection mentioned a Jordanian antiquities dealer from Amman named Ghasan Rihani (who died in 2001). Schøyen, in denying the Iraqi origin of his collection, also referred to the same Jordanian dealer as the previous owner: according to him, the Rihani family had had the items in their possession since 1965, and their ownership history goes back to 1935. Schøyen's claim was supported by a Jordanian export document presented as evidence in its Arabic original and an English translation (Figure 5.4).

The UCL investigation report uses the term 'on the balance of probabilities' to suggest that the bowls were looted from Iraq after Operation Desert Storm in 1991 (the First Gulf War). This removal of cultural heritage was in violation of Iraqi and international laws, including Iraq's first antiquities law, from 1924, granting the Iraqi state undisputed and sole ownership of all antiquities and banning any unauthorized export, as well as the international sanctions imposed on Iraq to prevent any form of commercial dealings with Iraq, let alone in sensitive items covered particularly by Security Council resolutions related to the protection of Iraq's cultural heritage. In its final verdict, the report simply advises UCL to return the Aramaic incantation bowls to their homeland in Iraq.

Australia:	Anonymous private collection (Ballarat, VIC)	1
France:	Private collection of Laurent Hebenstreit (Paris)	2
Germany:	Private collection of P. Kress (Bochum)	3
Iran:	National Museum of Iran (Teheran)	1
Iraq:	Iraq Museum (Baghdad)	4
	Sulaimaniah Museum (Sulaimaniah)	1
Israel:	Av private collection (Jerusalem)	4
Italy:	Banca d'Italia (Rome)	1
	Anonymous private collection (Rome)	2
Norway:	Private collection of Martin Schoyen (Oslo)	22
Spain:	Private collection (Barcelona)	1
	Private collection (Madrid)	2
USA:	Cornell University (Ithaca, NY)	1,465
	Green Collection (Oklahoma City, OK)	4
	Private collection of E. S. (unlocated)	3
	Private collection of M. Cohen (unlocated)	2
	Private collection of P. J. (unlocated)	2
	Anonymous private collection (San Francisco, CA)	2
	Anonymous private collection (unlocated)	95
Unknown country:	Anonymous private collections	8
Galleries, auction houses:	Archaeological Center (Tel Aviv-Jaffa, Israel)	1
	Drouot-Montaigne (Paris, France)	1
	eBay (San Jose, CA, USA)	1
Total texts:		*1,628*

Figure 5.4: English translation of Rihani export license.

Sources: Brodie (2017); Freeman et al. (2006: 14).

Scholarly views

- Martin Schøyen: 'By acquiring unprovenanced objects, I am "rescuing" them for historical research, thereby acting in the public good and promoting scholarship. [. . .] My collection might make a difference for the writing of history' (Westenholz 2010: 263).
- Shaul Shaked, in his interview with Samuel Thrope (2016),[11] stated clearly: 'As a scholar, I won't allow anything that has historical meaning and importance

11 Samuel Thrope is an American writer and translator based in Jerusalem. He has written for The Nation, the Daily Beast and Haaretz, among others. He published an article on

to rot in someplace and not touch it, or be destroyed because someone can't sell it. I think that it is a crime against humanity to allow this material to be lost. [. . .] A British person doesn't feel it very much. But Jews aren't allowed to enter certain parts of the world. And sometimes the things are connected to them personally – to their history and their tradition.' The bowls can be anywhere, as long as they allow access to the material.

- Mark Geller:[12] 'Within the past decade, hundreds of Aramaic incantation bowls have appeared on the antiquities market, collected from archaeological sites; there is no evidence that these objects have been stolen from a museum. As such, there is no identifiable owner. The Iraq Museum in Baghdad also houses a large collection of some 400 Aramaic incantation bowls, at last count, but few of these have ever been published. No Iraqi scholar has worked on them, nor has any Jewish or Israeli scholar been allowed to publish them. Someone from the UK has had permission to work on the Iraq Museum bowls, but so far there is no sign of publication, and they remain inaccessible to most scholars' (Geller 2005).
  'If the bowls were in Iraq, many of the leading scholars in the field, including Shaked, would no longer have access to them. Jewish scholars, Israeli or otherwise, have never been given permission to study the National Museum of Iraq's incantation bowls, the largest publicly owned collection in the world' (Brodie and Kersel 2014: 208).
- Colin Renfrew:[13] 'the tragedy is that all these incantation bowls would have contributed so much to knowledge and understanding if [the details of] their context and discovery had been known.' Renfrew and others also go further, saying that they shouldn't be studied. They argue that the study of these incantations, innocent as it might seem, is the last link in a chain of law-breaking that begins with looting, theft and cultural destruction (Freeman et al. 2006: 39).
- Neil Brodie:[14] 'We recognize the realities of the situation on the ground at the moment. We realise that this body of material is unusual: it's Jewish, not

---

the Schøyen Bowls and interviewed a group of scholars who clarified their true position on this topic, which has been used as a reference.

12 Professor Mark Geller, Head of UCL's Department of Hebrew and Jewish Studies when the bowls were first accepted on loan.

13 Colin Renfrew, senior fellow of the McDonald Institute for Archaeological Research at the University of Cambridge.

14 Neil J. Brodie, PhD from University of Liverpool, 1992, held positions at the British School at Athens; the University of Cambridge, where he was research director of the Illicit Antiquities Research Centre; and Stanford University's Archaeology Center, as

cuneiform tablets. There are questions hanging over its fate if it is returned to Iraq. Returning the bowls to Iraqi ownership does not necessarily mean returning them to Iraqi territory. They could be housed in an institution outside the country until the political situation improves – the British Museum, the Louvre and other institutions have offered to serve as safe havens for material from war zones – and until all researchers are granted access to them' (Brodie and Kersel 2014: 210).

Scholarly impact on monetary value

It is widely understood that the market value of unprovenanced antiquities significantly increases when either a scholar publishes a study or a museum exhibits them. In the case of the incantation bowls, it is expected that any such study would drive the price of the objects higher, and also create more demand for them. This in turn would lead to more destruction and looting at the site of origin, especially when the items are so important to certain faiths and can help reveal details related to a critical point of time.

Antiquity as 'surface finds'

Schøyen claimed that his bowls were 'chance/surface finds' (Brodie and Kersel 2014: 209). This claim was supported by statements from academics such as the following: 'Many of the sites in Iraq have Jewish Aramaic incantation bowls as surface finds, and these magic bowls date from the period of the Babylonian Talmud, c. 400–700 CE. These bowls reveal a great deal of useful social history about the Jewish community of Babylonia in late antiquity' (Geller 2005).

The first section of the statement tries to give the impression that those objects are in some way free for the public to pick up, and any absence of provenance should be acceptable because individuals might pick them up and keep them or even trade them at a later stage, without the need for any proper excavation work and archiving, as they have been found in the upper strata of most sites. But one could simply refer to the John Punnet Peters report from 1897, describing the findings in Nippur, which concludes that even items found at such surface locations would certainly contribute to a greater understanding of the site from

---

well as Senior Research Fellow in the Scottish Centre for Crime and Justice Research at the University of Glasgow.

spatial patterning and provide a clearer picture of the historical record of the site (Brodie and Kersel 2014: 209).

It is believed that the Schøyen bowls are now being studied by Siam Bhayro of the University of Exeter in the UK, which will surely add another chapter to this ongoing case.[15]

5.4 The Irisaĝrig cuneiform tablets

The Nabu Museum in northern Lebanon opened its gates in 2018, but it has already become the subject of a controversy over suspicions that some of the objects in its collection may have been illegally removed from Iraq. The museum's collection includes about 2,000 pieces that its owners have acquired since 1990 through direct purchase from different sources. These objects include a number of ancient Iraqi cuneiform clay tablets that cover a time span extending from the era of Sumerian city-states to the Middle Babylonian period (ca. 2600 to 1100 BCE).

Some 331 clay tablets have been officially studied by Owen, who published a study of them in two volumes, the first one (Owen et al. 2013). In it he documented his deciphering and translation of a total of 144 tablets. In the second volume he studied a total of 187 tablets. It was published in a separate volume (Lafont and Owen 2019), concerning tablets that were studied by Bertrand Lafont.[16]

Owen and Lafont's study reveals that the museum's collection includes about 135 clay tablets[17] that come from an archaeological site called Irisaĝrig, which has not yet been officially excavated and is thought to be in the central part of Iraq. This raises many questions about how the museum obtained this collection, including whether it is linked to a much larger collection containing thousands of ancient artefacts, including 250 cuneiform tablets from the Irisaĝrig site that was seized in the United States in 2016.[18] These objects were purchased by

15 See the University of Exeter website: *Research Projects: Pre-Islamic Incantation Bowl*, http://humanities.exeter.ac.uk/theology/research/projects/pre-islamic_incantation_bowls.

16 Bertrand Lafont, Assyriologist, Historian of Ancient Mesopotamia, Director of Research at the French National Centre for Scientific Research, Paris.

17 Collector/Owner: Jawad Adra/Nabu Museum, Lebanon. Scholar/Institution: David Owen/Cornell University, New York; Bertrand Lafont/French National Centre for Scientific Research, Paris.

18 The tablets were examined by Eckart Frahm of Yale University. See for example Arraf (2018), McGlone (2018); see also Emerson (2018) and Jarus (2018). At that same official ceremony, hundreds of other tablets from the Green Collection, also purchased by the Hobby Lobby Corporation in previous years, were ordered to be returned to Iraq.

Hobby Lobby Corporation for its Museum of the Bible in Washington, DC. The US Department of Justice had at that time determined that their provenance was Iraq. Another interesting case has just been revealed related to another scandal between an academic expert and the Bible Museum and Hobby Lobby Corporation (Moss 2019; Beaumont 2019).

The tablets from the ancient city of Irisaĝrig began to appear in academic publications and on the online market only a little later than the tablets from the Garšana archive. The first tablets from Irisaĝrig were published in 2002 by Giovanni De Sossi, and a tablet identified as one from Irisaĝrig was auctioned in 2004 on eBay. In 2005, Giovanni Pettinato published a catalogue of 166 tablets from Irisaĝrig (Menegazzi 2005: 79–98), tablets that had been confiscated by the Jordanian authorities in July 2003.[19] Unfortunately, many other tablets from Irisaĝrig escaped the attention of customs authorities and began to appear conspicuously on the Internet already in 2005. Figure 5.5 shows the cataloguing and publication of texts from Irisaĝrig.

In Owen's introduction to the Nabu Museum tablets, he clearly suggests that the clay cuneiform tablets in the Nabu Museum could have been looted from Iraq.[20] Some of the items suffered physical damage caused by poor storage and handling, which reflects the ignorance of thieves and smugglers. Iraq became a target for heavy looting after international sanctions were imposed on the country in the 1990s.

Scholarly views

David Owen and Bertrand Lafont: 'At a moment in time when the cultural legacy of Iraq and Syria is being devastated, it is particularly important that the scattered remnants of this destruction are recorded and published. We trust, that by providing this publication of the Adra Collection to a broader Lebanese public, it will also provide an exposure to the importance of its neighbour's rich history and culture and thereby join with the international community to help to protect their legacy' (Lafont and Owen 2019: 5).

Having failed to produce provenance information, official export licenses or customs declarations, the Nabu Museum owners are expected to return their cuneiform collection to Iraq. The other factor that supported Iraq's claim was

19 For more information on the 166 tablets seized by the Jordanian customs authorities, see Owen (2013).

20 'Many tablets were pastiches, created by the looters or dealers to represent complete tablets' (Lafont and Owen 2019: 7).

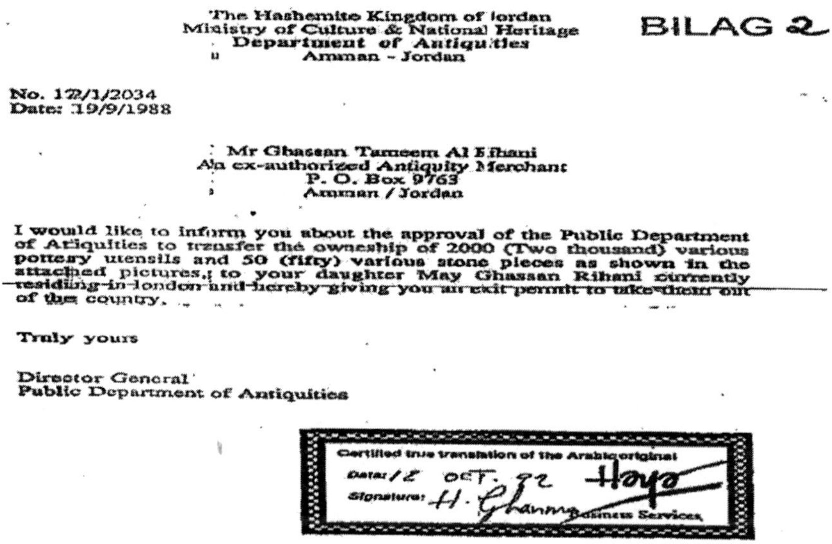
The Hashemite Kingdom of Jordan
Ministry of Culture & National Heritage
Department of Antiquities
Amman - Jordan

BILAG 2

No. 12/1/2034
Date: 19/9/1988

Mr Ghassan Tameem Al Rihani
An ex-authorized Antiquity Merchant
P. O. Box 9763
Amman / Jordan

I would like to inform you about the approval of the Public Department of Antiquities to transfer the ownership of 2000 (Two thousand) various pottery utensils and 50 (fifty) various stone pieces as shown in the attached pictures, to your daughter May Ghassan Rihani currently residing in london and hereby giving you an exit permit to take them out of the country.

Truly yours

Director General
Public Department of Antiquities

Certified true translation of the Arabic original
Date: 12 OCT. 92
Signature: H. Ghanma
Business Services

Figure 5.5: Cataloguing and publication of text from Irisaĝrig.
Source: Molina (2019: 9).

the proven fact that no registered excavations to this day have been conducted at the Irisaĝrig site.

5.5 The online antiquities trade

Following the First Gulf War in 1991, large quantities of unprovenanced cuneiform tablets started surfacing on the antiquities market and in private collections. Such tablets are found mainly, though not exclusively, in Iraq. A non-professional would not find it difficult to identify these artefacts, but would need an expert's assistance to read and translate the contents. Thus, some of the offered tablets have a note saying they could be sold with either the type of the content and also a translation prior to sale is included by means of an academic [optional] assistance.

In September 2008, 332 unprovenanced cuneiform tablets[21] were available for purchase on the Internet (Brodie 2011b), 211 of which had been translated by

21 Collector/Owner: Antiquities online shopping sites. Scholar/Institution: Wilfrid Lambert et al.

the prominent Assyriologist Wilfred Lambert.[22] In the same year, Lambert provided descriptions for thirty-two out of 142 cylinder seals offered for sale online. Most of the pieces that carry Lambert's authentication are unprovenanced, and Lambert's records themselves do not refer to the provenance.

David Owen published an article in 2009 in which he stated that between 2003 and 2008, he identified no fewer than 500 genuine cuneiform tablets on the Internet and also observed the presence of forged tablets (Owen 2009: 131, note 3).

Cuneiform reading and authentication services

A second strategy to assist with sales and to guard against fakes is the use of academics to authenticate material before sale. One website, the UK-based Collector Antiquities, went a step further, offering a 'cuneiform reading service', which includes translations of cuneiform texts by an academic Assyriologist for prices starting from 30 pounds.

The service terms could be tailored according to the particulars of each individual text, so that if it included anything of academic significance, the scholar could require that the purchaser allow the contents of the tablet to be included in any future publication. This means that the scholar involved with the service would benefit twice, once upon selling the translation with the tablet, and again with the opportunity to publish the content of the tablet as part of her or his academic work in the future.

Depending upon the nature of the tablet, the scholar might not need to physically investigate it and could simply use high-resolution photographs, which would not require any proof of purchase or title of ownership or provenance. This service could be extended to other objects as well to establish authenticity, such us cylinder seals. Other services on offer include how to distinguish between real and fake antiquities, with few lines explaining the advantage of buying such material from eBay, ensuring the highest confidence and trust!

Scholars have commented on the unprovenanced issue of objects in the following terms.

22 Wilfred Lambert is Professor Emeritus of Assyriology at Birmingham University (retired now), and a Fellow of the British Academy.

Scholarly views

- Wilfred Lambert: 'I don't necessarily know where it comes from or how long it's been coming', and the dealers 'don't themselves, I suspect, very often' (Gottlieb and Meier 2003b).
- Andrew George:[23] 'The undeniable importance of primary sources for the reconstruction of man's past makes it imperative that all cuneiform texts be published without prejudice, no matter what their origin, history, and present location, and whether or not their owner makes public what he knows of their recent history' (George 2009: xvi).

Currently there are still many tablets being sold online, mostly by private individuals. It is worth noting that some of them are described as 'souvenirs' from Iraq, from when their owners were there 'serving their country', which leads to the unavoidable conclusion that these objects were taken by a specific group of people present in Iraq in 2003 (such as the US Army) who were allowed to take antiquities with them upon their return home (Samuel 2018).

Conclusion

In his study published in 2019, Manuel Molina, a well-known Assyriologist based at the Spanish National Research Council in Madrid, makes a number of remarkable conclusions related to Ur III published tablets (Molina 2018: 233–62). Firstly, he confirms that the global number of Ur III texts catalogued in BDTNS (Owen 2013) since 1991 is quite remarkable: there are 56,809 texts, nearly all unprovenanced. If we consider that the total corpus of Ur III texts in BDTNS currently numbers 95,207 texts (November 2018), this means that 60 per cent of the Ur III corpus has been published since the First Gulf War in 1991. Secondly, Molina acknowledges the difficulty of identifying a single looted tablet either in publication or on the Internet before 1997. This fact would suggest that looting operations at Ur III sites were not undertaken immediately after the First Gulf War, but around the mid-1990s, when the economic embargo was at its

23 Professor Andrew George studied Assyriology at the University of Birmingham (1973–9) and for a while kept a public house in Darlaston. He wrote his doctoral dissertation on 'Babylonian Topographical Texts' under the supervision of Wilfred Lambert in 1985. Since 1983 he has taught Akkadian and Sumerian language and literature at SOAS, University of London, where he is now Professor of Babylonian Literature. See his profile on the SOAS website: https://www.soas.ac.uk/staff/staff30983.php.

most severe, and when the first looting episodes were actually reported (Stone 2008: 125–38).

Many scholars and experts have been mentioned in this chapter who feel no guilt about their conduct. As Neil Brodie puts it, 'the absence of provenance is not necessarily the same thing as illicit provenance and suspicion of theft is not knowledge of theft'. Thus, most of the academics involved are not concerned about whether they are doing anything illegal, or if they are actually unknowingly involved in some type of criminal activity.

UCL launched a new policy in June 2009 regarding the risks involved in working with cultural property. It basically highlights the reputational risks, but does not address the possible criminal associations involved in such activities, which could pose a risk to the staff's reputation in the future (Brodie and Kersel 2014: 208).

Beyond the issue of scholarly publications and studies, conclusions can be drawn from the details of each case presented. The illicit antiquities trade is helped by at least three means of support directly provided by scholars' involvement: (a) a scholar's involvement in identifying the artefact contributes to a price increase; (b) a scholar's identification of an object promotes market trust and confidence; and (c) suppression of an object's provenance prevents any investigation.

The nature of the current debate over academia's involvement is mainly ethical: this may be because matters relating to cultural heritage and antiquity are considered purely human based subjects, there is no direct physical side to it (Brew 2001: 103).

Despite the fact that unlawful dealing in cultural heritage objects can cause harm, one has to admit that such harm has always been justified by the parties involved in illicit trade, such as dealers, collectors, museums and academics, by claiming that their noble goal has always been the safeguarding of public knowledge and art (Cuno 2009). Such justifications certainly encourage well-off collectors, both individuals and institutions, who know there will be some sort of safety blanket to protect their interests if things go wrong. Hence, we see many obstacles arising to any attempted investigation (Felch and Frammolino 2011; Gross 2009; Watson and Todeschini 2007), which is one of the reasons why the Iraqi State Board of Antiquities and Heritage is reluctant to pursue legal action against some collectors: they know that it would require top-notch legal advisers to challenge the collector's consortium of high-powered lawyers, a process that could well take years to settle and would represent a heavy financial burden.

Today we see evidence of a global recognition of the serious risks facing cultural heritage thanks to the wide attention it is getting from international agencies focusing on the problem (e.g., the 1970 UNESCO Convention on the

Means of Prohibiting and Preventing the Illicit Import, Export and Transfer of Ownership of Cultural Property; the 1995 UNIDROIT Convention on Stolen or Illegally Exported Cultural Objects; and the 2007 UN Declaration on the Rights of Indigenous Peoples, which recognizes the rights of indigenous peoples to control the past, present and future manifestations of their culture, including cultural objects). The 2000 UN Convention against Transnational Organized Crime covers any small group of people (three or more) working jointly over a period of time committing serious transnational crimes that directly or indirectly have financial or other material benefit. This description of such crimes could well be applied to some of the cases discussed in this study, which has identified a hierarchy of systems, causing an increase in demand in the antiquities market. Given that academics' services are at the very core of it, they should be made aware of the legal implications involved in working with collectors and dealers who trade in unprovenanced material.

Ethnic and cultural identities are all connected, thus any loss in any of their components causes a damage beyond academic involvement, any destruction or looting that takes place at archaeological sites could simply break the sensitive continuous chain of knowledge and cause confusion in our understanding to their identities (Brodie 2011b).

Acknowledgements

The author thanks Neil Brodie for his unwavering help and constructive suggestions. He would also like to thank Abdul Ameer Al-Hamdani for his valuable advice and support, and Nadia Ait Said-Ghanem, who has reviewed the chapter and assisted with her insightful remarks.

References

Arraf, Jane (2018), 'Hobby Lobby's Illegal Antiquities Shed Light On a Lost, Looted Ancient City in Iraq', in *WNIN*, 28 June 2018, https://news.wnin.org/node/65000

Aruz, Joan Ronald Wallenfels, eds (2003), *Art of the First Cities: The Third Millennium B.C. from the Mediterranean to the Indus*, New York, Metropolitan Museum of Art / New Haven/London, Yale University Press

Beaumont, Peter (2019), 'Oxford Professor Accused of Selling Ancient Bible Fragments', in *The Guardian*, 16 October, https://gu.com/p/cgt38

Brew, Angela (2001), *The Nature of Research. Inquiry in Academic Contexts*, London/New York, Routledge Falmer

Brodie, Neil (2008), 'The Market Background to the April 2003 Plunder of the Iraq National Museum', in Peter G. Stone Joanne Farchakh Bajjaly, eds, *The Destruction of Cultural Heritage in Iraq*, Woodbridge, Boydell Press, p. 41–54, https://traffickingculture.org/?p=554

Brodie, Neil (2011a), 'Congenial Bedfellows? The Academy and the Antiquities Trade', in *Journal of Contemporary Criminal Justice*, Vol. 27, No. 4, p. 408–437, https://traffickingculture.org/?p=545

Brodie, Neil (2011b), 'The Market in Iraqi Antiquities 1980–2009 and Academic Involvement in the Marketing Process', in Stefano Manacorda and Duncan Chappell, eds, *Crime in the Art and Antiquities World. Illegal Trafficking in Cultural Property*, New York, Springer, p. 117–133,https://traffickingculture.org/?p=546

Brodie, Neil (2017), 'The Rihani "Provenance"', in *Market of Mass Destruction*, 8 May, http://www.marketmassdestruction.com/the-rihani-provenance

Brodie, Neil J. and Morag M. Kersel (2014), 'WikiLeaks, Text, and Archaeology: The Case of the Schoyen Incantation', in Matthew T. Rutz Morag M. Kersel, eds, *Archaeologies of Text. Archaeology, Technology, and Ethics*, Oxford/Philadelphia, Oxbow Books, p. 198–213

Brodie, Neil, Jennifer Doole and Colin Renfrew, eds (2001), *Trade in Illicit Antiquities. The Destruction of the World's Archaeological Heritage*, Cambridge, McDonald Institute for Archaeological Research

Brodie, Neil et al., eds (2006), *Archaeology, Cultural Heritage, and the Antiquities Trade*, Gainesville, University Press of Florida

Cuno, James (2009), 'Introduction', in James Cuno, ed., *Whose Culture? The Promise of Museums and the Debate over Antiquities*, Princeton/Oxford, Princeton University Press, p. 1–35

De Sossi, Giovanni (2002), 'One More šu-ba-ti Ur III Tablet', in *NABU. Nouvelles assyriologiques breves et utilitaires*, Vol. 4, No. 79 (December), p. 74–75

Emerson, Sarah (2018), 'Ancient Artifacts Smuggled by Hobby Lobby Traced to Mysterious Sumerian City', in *VICE*, 1 May, https://www.vice.com/en_us/article/paxnqn/ancient-artifacts-smuggled-by-hobby-lobby-traced-to-mysterious-sumerian-city-irisagrig-mesopotamian

Felch, Jason and Ralph Frammolino (2011), *Chasing Aphrodite. The Hunt for Looted Antiquities at the World's Richest Museum*, Boston/New York, Houghton Mifflin Harcourt

Finkel, Irving (2004), 'Perspective of an Academic', in Matt Kimmich, ed., *Not For Sale. A Swiss–British Conference on the Traffic in Artefacts from Iraq, Afghanistan and Beyond*, Bern, British Council, p. 41–42

Freeman, David John, Sally McDonal and Colin Renfrew (2006), *An Inquiry into the Provenance of 654 Aramaic Incantation Bowls Delivered into the Possession of UCL by, or on the Instruction of, Mr. Martin Schøyen*, Inquiry established by the Provost of UCL, https://www.wikileaks.org/wiki/UK_possession_of_art_works_looted_from_Iraq:_Schoyen_UCL_Inquiry_report%2C_2009

Geller, Mark (2005), 'Spies, Thieves and Cultural Heritage', in *UCL Institute of Jewish Studies News*, http://web.archive.org/web/20051120112340/http://www.ucl.ac.uk/hebrew-jewish/ijs/news.htm

George, Andrew R. (2009), *Babylonian Literary Texts in the Schøyen Collection*, Bethesda, CDL Press

Gottlieb, Martin and Barry Meier (2003a), 'Ancient Art at Met Raises Old Ethical Questions', in *The New York Times*, 2 August, https://www.nytimes.com/2003/08/02/world/ancient-art-at-met-raises-old-ethical-questions.html

Gottlieb, Martin and Barry Meier (2003b), 'Of 2,000 Treasures Stolen in Gulf War of 1991, Only 12 Have Been Recovered', in *The New York Times*, 1 May. http://www.nytimes.com/2003/05/01/world/aftereffects-plunder-2000-treasures-stolen-gulf-war-1991-only-12-have-been.html

Gross, Michael (2009), *Rogues' Gallery. The Secret History of the Moguls and the Money that Made the Metropolitan Museum*, New York, Broadway Books

Hansen, Donald P. (2002), "Through the Love of Ishtar", in Lamia al-Gailani Werr et al., eds, Of Pots and Plans. Papers on the Archaeology and History of Mesopotamia and Syria Presented to David Oates in Honour of His 75th Birthday, London, Nabu, p. 91–112

Hansen, Donald P. (2003), 'Art of the Akkadian Dynasty', in Joan Aruz RonaldWallenfels, eds, *Art of the First Cities: The Third Millennium B.C. from the Mediterranean to the Indus*, New York, Metropolitan Museum of Art / New Haven/London, Yale University Press, p. 189–209

Institute of Fine Arts (2007), *Donald P. Hansen, 1931–2007. In Memoriam*, 16 February, https://www.nyu.edu/gsas/dept/fineart/pdfs/press/Hansen_memoriam.pdf

Janus, Owen (2018), 'Stolen Sumerian Tablets Come from the Lost City of Irisagrig', in *Live Science*, 30 April 2018, https://www.livescience.com/62437-stolen-sumerian-tablets-from-lost-city.html

Lafont, Bertrand and David I. Owen (2019), *From Mesopotamia to Lebanon. The Jawad Adra Cuneiform Collection in the Nabu Museum at El Heri, Lebanon*, S.l., Penn State University Press, https://lily-triangle-95s7.squarespace.com/s/FROM-MESOPOTAMIA-TO-LEBANON-7mhk.pdf

Layard, Austen H. (1853), *Discoveries in the Ruins of Nineveh and Babylon*, New York, G.P. Putnam, https://archive.org/details/discoveriesinru00layagoog

McGlone, Peggy (2018), 'Hobby Lobby's Illicit Artifacts Are Returned to Their Iraqi Homeland', in *The Washington Post*, 2 May, https://www.washingtonpost.com/entertainment/museums/hobby-lobbys-illicit-artifacts-are-returned-to-their-iraqi-homeland/2018/05/02/3f59842a-4e44-11e8-84a0-458a1aa9ac0a_story.html

Menegazzi, Roberta, ed. (2005), *An Endangered Cultural Heritage. Iraqi Antiquities Recovered in Jordan*, Florence, Le Lettere

Molina, Manuel (2019), 'The Looting of UR III Tablets after the Gulf Wars. An Assessment', in Walter Sommerfield, ed., *Dealing with Antiquity: Past, Present & Future. Proceedings of the 63rd Recontre Assyriologique Internationale* (*Alter Orient und Altes Testament* 460), p. 233–262

Moss, Candida (2019), 'Hobby Lobby Scandal Widens as Museum of the Bible Admits Oxford Prof Sold Illicit Papyri to Green Family', in *The Daily Beast*, 14 October, https://www.thedailybeast.com/hobby-lobby-scandal-widens-as-museum-of-the-bible-admits-oxford-prof-sold-illicit-papyri-to-green-family

Owen, David I. (2007a), 'Acknowledgments', in David I. Owen and Rudolf H. Mayr, eds, *The Garšana Archives*, Bethesda, CDL Press, p. vii-ix

David I. Owen Rudolf H.Mayr, eds, *The Garšana Archives*, Bethesda, CDL Press

Owen, David I. (2007b), 'Series Editor's Preface', in David I.Owen Rudolf H. Mayr, eds, *The Garšana Archives*, Bethesda, CDL Press, p. v-vi

Owen, David I. (2009), 'Censoring Knowledge: The Case for the Publication of Unprovenanced Cuneiform Tablets', in James Cuno, ed., *Whose Culture? The Promise of Museums and the Debate over Antiquities*, Princeton/Oxford, Princeton University Press, p. 125–142

Owen, David I. (2013), *Nisaba 15/2*, in *Database of Neo-Sumerian Texts* (BDTNS), https://tinyurl.com/y78v9jxh

Owen, David I. et al. (2013), *Cuneiform Texts Primarily from Iri-Saĝrig/Āl-Šarrākī and the History of the Ur III Period. Vol. 1: Commentary and Indexes* (Nisaba 15/1), Bethesda, CDL Press

Owen, David I. et al. (2013), *Cuneiform Texts Primarily from Iri-Saĝrig/Āl-Šarrākī and the History of the Ur III Period. Vol. 2: Catalogue and Texts* (Nisaba 15/2), Bethesda, CDL Press

Peters, John P. (1897), *Nippur, or, Explorations and Adventures on the Euphrates. The Narrative of the University of Pennsylvania Expedition to Babylonia in the Years 1888–1890*, New York, G.P. Putnam, https://archive.org/details/nippurorexplorat01pete

Samuel, Sigal (2018), 'It's Disturbingly Easy to Buy Iraq's Archeological Treasures', in *The Atlantic*, 19 March, https://www.theatlantic.com/international/archive/2018/03/iraq-war-archeology-invasion/555200

Shaked, Shaul (2001), 'Jews, Christians and Pagans in the Aramaic Incantation bowls of the Sassanid Period', in Adriana Destro Mauro Pesce, eds, *Religions and Cultures. First International Conference of Mediterraneum*, Binghamton, Global Publications Binghamton University, p. 61–67

Shaked, Shaul, James Nathan Ford and Siam Bhayro (2013), *Aramaic Bowl Spells. Jewish Babylonian Aramaic Bowls, Volume 1*, Leide/Boston, Brill, https://archive.org/details/AramaicBowlSpellsJewishBabylonianAramaicBowls

Stone, Elizabeth C. (2008), 'Patterns of Looting in Southern Iraq', in *Antiquity*, Vol. 82, No. 315 (March), p. 125–138

Stone, Elizabeth C. (2015), 'An Update on the Looting of Archaeological Sites in Iraq', in *Near Eastern Archaeology*, Vol. 78, No. 3, p. 178–186

Thrope, Samuel (2016), 'Magic Bowls of Antiquity', in *Aeon*, 24 May, https://aeon.co/essays/what-should-be-done-with-the-magic-bowls-of-jewish-babylonia

Vrdoljak, Ana Filipa (2006), *International Law, Museums and the Return of Cultural Objects*, Cambridge, Cambridge University Press, p. 261–273

Watson, Peter and Cecilia Todeschini (2007), *The Medici Conspiracy. The Illicit Journey of Looted Antiquities from Italy's Tomb Raiders to the World's Greatest Museums*, New York, PublicAffairs

Westenholz, Aage (2010), 'Illicit Cuneiform Tablets: Heirlooms or Stolen Goods?', in Alexandra Kleinerman and Jack M. Sasson, eds, *Why Should Someone Who Knows Something Conceal It? Cuneiform Studies in Honor of David I. Owen on his 70th Birthday*, Bethesda, CDL Press, p. 257–272

Lorenzo Kamel

Chapter 6: Cultural Heritage as a Process of Accumulation: The 'Paradigm of Gilgamesh'

Cultural heritage is not only a relatively new idea – deeply rooted in the 19th century, when Europeans showed an increasing interest in preserving Medieval buildings – but also a problematic one. It is, in fact, a top-down ideal usually defined by the most powerful members of society. To counter this, a number of interested observers have stressed the need to democratize cultural heritage, giving greater control to local communities. This chapter contends that the 'democratization' of cultural heritage should be coupled, on a more theoretical level, with a process of 'de-Westernization' that builds on a more informed awareness about the process of 'accumulation' which underpins many of the achievements, ideals and perceptions that lie at the very base of much of what we commonly consider as tangible (such as works of art, artefacts, books) and intangible culture (such as knowledge, folklore, and traditions).

Some scholars have claimed that 'Cultural heritage is a Western construct' (Smallacombe 2000: 156), 'a Western term',[1] and 'a Western product linked to the birth of modernity' (Vicente Rabanaque 2015: 95). Yet, in order to understand and/or deconstruct these claims, it is not sufficient to stick to what we commonly refer to as 'cultural heritage'. It is indeed necessary to go back to its very roots, providing a non-Western understanding of what lies beneath and around our shared heritage.

6.1 Beyond Eurocentrism

What does imperialism mean? In 1878, British statesman Robert Lowe (1811–1892) answered as follows: 'It means the assertion of absolute force over others' (Lowe (1878: 458). 140 years later historian Emilio Gentile made recourse to the concept of *mondialità* (globality) to describe many of the effects of this same absolute power, understood by him in reference to the apex of 'European globality' in the late 19th century, as the 'effective military, political, economic and cultural supremacy exerted by one human collective over other peoples on

1 'Ali 'Oshaish cited in Lamprakos (2015: 136).

the planet, legitimating it via a belief in itself as a universal civilisation destined to model and guide humanity as a whole' (Gentile 2018: 4).

Many of the geographical contexts mentioned in this volume and, in particular, in this chapter, have experienced various forms of European 'globality', prompting a number of eminent scholars to agree with Johan Huizinga's thesis (1872–1945) according to which 'our [European] civilization is the first to have for its past the past of the world' (Huizinga 1936: 8).[2] It should be clarified that these arguments were not new even at the time. Amongst other intellectuals, for example, Antonio Gramsci (1891–1937) noted that 'other cultures' have had 'universal value only in so far as they have become constituent elements of European culture, which is the only historically and concretely universal culture – in so far, that is, as they have contributed to the process of European thought and been assimilated by it'.[3] There is thus nothing surprising about the fact that, in the years and decades which followed, a large number of historians argued that they felt no need, to cite Hugh Trevor-Roper (1914–2003), 'to make any apology if our study of history is Eurocentric', in the sense that 'It is European techniques, European examples, European ideas which have shaken the non-European world out of its past' (Trevor-Roper 1965: 11).[4]

These arguments, in common with a plethora of other similar claims, can be traced in various forms and to various extents to what Peter Burke (1998: 2) has called 'the grand narrative' of the affirmation of Western civilisation, delineated in terms of a 'a *triumphalist account of Western* achievement from the *Greeks onwards* in which the Renaissance is a link in a chain which includes the Reformation, the Scientific Revolution, the Enlightenment, the Industrial Revolution and so on'.[5] Each of these historical periods has been (and often still is) frequently presented by juxtaposing an alleged European activism with a supposed intrinsic 'Oriental' passivity. 'The last great non-European navigator to venture onto the oceans in search of new lands', noted, among others, Gentile (2018: 8–9), 'was [from 1403 to 1433] Muslim Chinaman Zheng He [. . .] In the

---

2 According to Tagliaferri (2019: 25), Huizinga's thesis can be to some extent supported 'if we do not allow ourselves to be overly intimated by political correctness concerns'.

3 Notebook 15 (1933), para. 61. See Gramsci 1971: 416.

4 Eric L. Jones (1981) devoted the lion's share of his book to explaining the presumed reasons for which Europeans alone have been capable of understanding and enjoying 'freedom'.

5 Burke (1998:2) considers European culture as just one among others, coexisting and interacting with its neighbours, notably Byzantium and Islam both of which had their own 'Renaissances' of Greek and Roman antiquity.

succeeding four centuries, it was European navigators alone who took to the oceans in search of new routes and lands'.[6]

Despite the success and widespread dissemination of the 'triumphalist account', it is important to highlight the existence of an underlying misconception common to Huizinga, Gramsci and Trevor-Roper – or at least the way in which their 'universalist' theories have frequently been interpreted – and the numerous scholars who still today subscribe to a certain way of approaching the role historically played by Europe. The origins of the bulk of the 'positive'[7] and foundational elements to 'European universalism' can hardly be linked only, or mainly, to Europe. Critical thought, freedom of research, experimental science, secular culture and politics, the sovereignty of the people, looking after the elderly and many other aspects and phenomena encompassed by a number of scholars into 'European globality' are indeed part of a complex human history – which, according to Hegelian tradition,[8] 'others' were not fully able to understand – largely written and shaped away from the Old Continent.

Jack Goody (1919–2015) noted that Europe 'makes many claims to having invented a range of value-laden institutions such as "democracy", mercantile "capitalism", freedom, individualism. However, these institutions are found over a much more widespread range of human societies' (Goody 2006: 1).[9] His words are even more pertinent if considering that an ongoing *world* economy existed

6 According to Blaut (2000: 130), 'For Eurocentric historians, the important thing about Zheng He's voyages is not that they took place – representing perhaps the greatest ocean exploit in human history up to that time – but that they stopped'.

7 European globality's 'negative' elements are frequently seen as encompassing 'imperialism, racism, exploitation of subject peoples and even genocide'. According to some scholars, the positive aspects of European globality are 'more numerous' than its negatives. See Detti 2019: 71.

8 Whilst acknowledging the great contribution made by 'others' to astronomy, grammar, algebra and many other fields, Hegel was convinced that non-European peoples were lacking tools with which to understand history. In his words: 'Though the recent discoveries of the treasures of Indian Literature have shown us what a reputation the Hindoos have acquired in Geometry, Astronomy, and Algebra – that they have made great advances in Philosophy, [...] – we find the department of History altogether neglected, or rather non-existent. For History requires Understanding – the power of looking at an object in an independent objective light, and comprehending it in its rational connection with other objects' (Hegel 1956 [1837]: 161–2).

9 Goody (2006: 51) notes that 'there is no sense in which the Greeks can be said to have "discovered individual freedom" or democracy'.

before the Europeans had much to do and say in it (Frank 1998: xxiv).[10] More specifically:

> Africa, Asia, and Europe shared equally in the rise of capitalism prior to 1492. After that date, Europe took the lead. This happened [. . .] because of Europe's location near America and because of the immense wealth obtained by Europeans in America and later in Asia and Africa – not because Europeans were brighter or bolder or better than non-Europeans, or more modern, more advanced, more progressive, more rational. These are myths of Eurocentric diffusionism [. . .] (Blaut 1993: 206).[11]

All this is not intended at downsizing the role played by European 'activism' or its impact. It is enough here to mention, for instance, that the lion's share of the names frequently still used today for many post-colonial spaces bears direct witness to what the Old Continent appropriated during the 'European globality' or the historical phases which prepared the way for it. Think of Pau Brasil (Brazil), the Gold Coast (Ghana), the Silver River (Rio de la Plata), Land

---

10 In Frank's words: 'If any regions were predominant in the world economy before 1800, they were in Asia' (Frank 1998: 5). Frank's words are of particular significance, above, all in the context of the innovations which were later at the heart of the first Industrial Revolution (1760–1820). Think, for example, of the radical technological and military strategy and tactics changes in Europe from 1560 to the middle of the 17th century. The origins of the elements behind this very 'military revolution' were rooted in Asia. The invention of gunpowder around the 10th century originated with a Chinese invention and was imported to Europe in the centuries which followed thanks to a sort of osmosis process which encompassed China itself, the Arab world and the West. Even the so-called Heilongjiang cannon dates to China in 1288 where exploding mines, metal bullets and the earliest rudimentary missiles were invented in these same years. The same can be said of all the sectors which acted as the driving forces behind the first Industrial Revolution. Think of the 'burning stones', which Marco Polo (1254–1324) wrote of in *Milione* in reference to coal and, more generally, to China's pioneering fossil fuels. Machines for the working of silk and cotton thread, iron and steel production, the rudiments of steam engine building: we owe the invention of all of these tools to an 'Oriental' legacy and the genius of people like Arab mechanic Al-Jazarī (1136–1206) and Chinese inventor Wang Zhen (1290–1333). These were later developed and applied systematically in Europe, as was the case of the application of steam engines to the transport and industry sectors by James Watt (1736–1819), for example.

11 Cyril L.R. James, of Trinidad, noted in his famous study of the 1791 Haiti revolution that 'the slave-trade and slavery were the economic basis of the French revolution [. . .] Nearly all the industries which developed in France during the eighteenth century had their origin in goods or commodities destined either for the coast of Guinea or for America' (James 1989: 47–8). The first constituent assembly in French history, in 1790, stated that slavery was 'essential to French prosperity'.

of Silver (Argentina), Costa Ricca (Costa Rica), the Ivory Coast, the Spice Islands (the Maluku islands), Black (Niger), Black Land (Nigeria), but also Sudan, which derives from the Arabic 'land of the Blacks' reminding us that some of the peoples and ethnic groups who have most suffered the consequences of modern slavery are themselves bound up with a past whose roots frequently lie in the systematic exploitation of millions of slaves[12]. In other cases, the names of these spaces are bound up with ongoing efforts by colonisers to obliterate the history of their subject peoples: for instance, no Indian Ocean existed prior to colonisation (the original name was 'Eritrean Sea') and the same is true of the Victoria Falls (*Mosi-oa-Thunya* in Lozi language 'the smoke which thunders') and the Gulf of Aden (Gulf of Berbera). Colombia (from Christopher Columbus), the Philippines (from Philip II of Spain) and many other countries mentioned in this chapter are the result of 'tributes' by those who came from 'outside' to the people who had made these conquests possible and the exploitation of peoples and local resources which resulted from these.

6.2 'Curiosity': a historic parallel

It may be of interest to trace now a parallel between the previous section's analysis and a historical debate which followed on from the publication, in the 1980s, of a series of books by renowned British historian Bernard Lewis (1916–2018). The latter argued that 'intellectual curiosity' as regards 'other cultures' – and thus the predisposition and will to study languages, history and traditions – is 'still peculiar to Western Europe, and to the inheritors and emulators of the European scholarly tradition' (Lewis 1993: 123–4). For Lewis, it was thus natural to claim that it is only with the European Renaissance that 'a human society for the first time developed the sophistication, the detachment and, above, all, the curiosity to study and appreciate the literary achievements of alien and even hostile societies' (Lewis 1982: 75).

Over the course of the years these arguments have been espoused by dozens of scholars, many of whom have applied it to specific contests and 'cultures'.

12 From 650 to the 19th century, the Arabs removed over 9 million African slaves from the continent, especially towards Arabia and neighbouring regions but also, in smaller numbers, to India and the Far East. An indirect confirmation of this is to be found in *Ta'rīkh al-rusul wa l-mulūk* (History of the Prophets and the Kings), the manuscript in which Tabarī described the Zanj Rebellion, a bloody revolt triggered in Basra (Southern Iraq) by black slaves originally from Africa from 869 to 883. It involved the whole region and created serious problems for the Abbasid Caliphate.

Franco Cardini went so far to claim that 'disinterest for civilisations other than Islamic ones' is 'a characteristic of the culture which emerged from Muhammad's religious revolution' (Cardini 2001: 23).

In more recent times, a wide range of new studies has demonstrated this argument's inherent baselessness and apparent solipsism in an increasingly accurate and well-documented way. I am referring, for example, to Roxanne L. Euben's studies, which have supplied a wide range of examples in support of the 'curiosity' and contributions offered by 'others' to phenomena encompassed by Gentile under 'European globality' (Euben 2006), as well as the work of Sanjay Subramanyam, – attentive, among other things, to highlight the dangers of conceiving of 'Europe as a *deus ex machina*' (Subramanyam 2019: 13)[13] – Pankaj Mishra (2012) – interested in the 19th century minds which moulded Asia and neighbouring continents – and Nabil Matar (2003), who has thrown light on the writings of 17th century Arab travellers and their curiosity as well as their ability to appreciate 'un-Islamic' concepts and aspects.

The social sciences have emerged as a response to what were perceived as 'European problems' (Wallerstein 1997: 21), contributing to casting light on the reasons behind the fact that the contributions of, and dynamics linked to, 'others' have long been absent from modern narratives, and often remain so today. To this it should be added, as Nizar F. Hermes (2012: 5) has noted in relation to the specific Mediterranean context, that 'the problem lies more in the Western neglect of the medieval corpus of Arabic writings about the Other'. In other words, a certain approach toward social sciences, coupled with a limited knowledge of complex languages and a plethora of manuscripts and documents produced in places which are still difficult to access today, have erroneously prompted a number of scholars to focus on a intrinsically innate absence of 'curiosity', that was presumed to characterize the 'others' (see also König 2015).[14]

This latter misunderstanding can in many ways be extended to the aspects mentioned at the beginning of this chapter. Just as 'curiosity' in regard to 'others' can in no way be considered exclusive to the history of European countries, similarly the critical thought and many other elements cited as part of what many consider to be a sort of 'European exceptionalism' should be traced back to a wider

---

13 On the way that a large part of European historiography suffers from a sort of amnesia in relation to the history of other cultures, see Subrahmanyam 2015: 444.

14 König (2015: 16) noted that 'distinguished international scholars have had no qualms to reduce a large and differentiated range of Arabic-Islamic perceptions to a single basic pattern which is often subsumed under the keywords "ignorance", "indifference", and "arrogance"'.

legacy (see Sen 2003 and Goody 1996), one which many of those living in what is now Europe in the Early Modern and pre-modern period drew from extensively.[15] As one of the many possible examples, think of celebrated Pisan mathematician Fibonacci (c.1175–c.1250), who studied for many years in the Algerian city of Béjaïa, focusing in particular on algebra (a word deriving from a written text by Persian mathematician Abū Ja'far Muhammad ibn Mūsā al-Khwārizmī, 780–850), as well as on arithmetic procedures used by local Arab (Muslims, Jews and Christians) scholars. Taking advantage from his intimate knowledge of Arabic, Fibonacci succeeded in introducing the decimal system into Europe together with the '*zephyrus*' concept, from Arabic *sifr*, which, in the pre-Islamic era meant 'empty' or 'zero'. The universal scope of discoveries linked to numbers and other aspects of human knowledge is thus not a mirror to the universalism of 'European culture' but rather confirms, once more, the 'universal value' of a complex human history cemented by knowledge accumulated in extremely variegated contexts, places and cultures. Note that the above arguments are also relevant to sub-Saharan Africa (especially Ethiopia, Chad, Tanzania and Senegal) which, although frequently perceived as one of the world's least evolved areas in cultural terms, was the cradle of some of the oldest, richest and most emulated literary traditions in the world (see Phillipson 2012, Munro-Hay 1991, Henze 2000). This latter aspect can in turn be extended to dozens of other cases and contexts – Japan, India and China included – to the extent that Gregor Paul (1993:120) was prompted to argue that 'so-called (traditional) "European" or "Western" logic, that is, Aristotelian syllogistic, and "Chinese" logic are basically the same'.[16] A greater awareness of these aspects can help to deconstruct and/or defuse many of the dynamics cutting through our present whilst also challenging what Christof Dejung, David Motadel and Jürgen Osterhammel (2019: 39) have defined 'notions of civilizational and cultural boundaries'.

---

15 On the matter of key contributions to 'experimental science' see, among other possible examples, the role of Damascus astronomer Taqī al-Dīn (1526–1585). On the process by which 'Ancient Egyptians discovered Algol's variability 3,000 years before Western astronomers', see Porceddu et al. (2018). Goody (1996: 38) has, for example, noted that 'in the ninth century we have an example of the application of the principle of *eiusdem generis* (interpreting a general term in a more specific way like other terms in the context), supposed only to have developed in Western common law in the nineteenth century'.

16 Paul (1993:120) has also demonstrated that whilst Aristotelian and 'classic' Indian logics 'developed independently, they are basically equivalent'.

6.3 The Gilgamesh paradigm

The underlying 'misunderstanding' referred to at the outset of this chapter can ultimately be traced to a widespread tendency to ignore or minimise anything which does not fit into the 'triumphalist account' referred to by Burke. In this respect, an especially significant aspect which we have not yet touched on derives from a largely successful attempt to detach the ancient Greek legacy from its Mediterranean and 'oriental' association.[17]

In what is now Lebanon, the Phoenicians 'had something comparable to the self-regulating city-state or polis' and there is archaeological and historical evidence to support the thesis by which the origins of some of the 'Greek political arrangements we most admire' are to be traced to the Phoenicians (Hornblower 1992: 2). The Tell el-'Amarna's Letters, whose corpus consists of 382 tablets inscribed in cuneiform characters in around the 14th century BCE, document the existence of Phoenician towns 'ruled, at least from time to time, by deliberative forums of a broad cross-section of the citizens' (Stockwell 2010: 127). 6th century BCE Tyre, on the coast in what is now Lebanon, was 'a republic headed by elective magistrates' (Bondi 2001: 153). According Stephan Stockwell (2010: 129), the Phoenicians could count on what we would consider today a 'proto-democracy':

> The Phoenicians brought more than just trade into the Greek sphere and they could have quite possibly had a formative influence on Greek political institutions that resulted in democratic configurations equivalent to Kleisthenes's reforms. Athenian democracy was a complex set of interlocking institutions with regular meetings. There is some evidence that at least Byblos, Sidon, Tyre, Sparta and Chios can match this formulation. (Stockwell 2010: 133)

These and many other possible examples are not intended to suggest that the Phoenicians, the Carthaginians (who, for Greek historian Polybius, achieved much higher 'proto-democratic' standards than the Romans[18]), the Indians and other peoples and civilisations 'invented' democracy but rather that the practices and principles underlying the latter – like many other aspects tracing back to the driving forces underlying the rise of 'European globality' – are the result of an all too frequently ignored or silenced accumulation process.

---

17 According to Peter K.J. Park (2013: 126), 'The East is not the West because the East lacks what is essentially Western: the "principle of *individual freedom*," which is dominant in the "Greek element"'.

18 Polybius (206 BCE–118 BCE) noted that 'the multitude at Carthage had already acquired the chief voice in deliberations' while in Rome only 'the most eminent men' were consulted. See Polybius 1923: 385.

The issue of ancient Greece's 'oriental' legacy also fits into this analysis. To cite Ellen Meiksins Wood's words (1942–2016), 'it is even more artificial to detach ancient Greece from, say, Egypt or Persia, as if the Greeks were always "European", living a separate history, and not part of a larger Mediterranean and "Eastern" world' (Meiksins Wood 2011: 26). In other words, those linking Europe with Ancient Greece and thus to many of the previously mentioned concepts and ideas are simply – more or less consciously – recognising Europe's oriental roots (in Greek mythology, Europe refers to Agenor's, king of Tyre's daughter, in modern day Lebanon) and its dominant religion (Christianity was an oriental religion). In John M. Hobson's words:

> Eurocentric scholars assume that the rise of capitalist modernity was pioneered solely by the Europeans without any help from the Easterners. [. . .]. Deconstructing Eurocentrism [. . .] enables us to reveal the European West as a *hybrid* entity that has been shaped by the East [. . .]. Today we take it as axiomatic that Greece was the birthplace of Europe. For it was there where science and rational thinking were allegedly first established, only to be reclaimed after the Dark Age interlude during the so-called Italian Renaissance. But this notion of Greece is a fabrication – an idea that was constructed by European thinkers only as late as the end of the eighteenth century [. . .]. Greece was linked spiritually and culturally to the East [. . .]. Moreover, that Ancient Greece owes so much to ancient Egypt (as the Greeks readily acknowledged), wreaks havoc with the notion of a pure Aryan lineage of Europe that is cherished by Eurocentric thinkers. (Hobson 2006: 109–110)

These considerations are also bound up with the misleading perception that is frequently referred to as the 'Western Jewish-Christian tradition'. This latter is still today habitually referred to by scholars as 'the cradle of principles of equality and justice' (Amato and Cardia 2015: 597), while others focus on 'democracy's biblical roots' (Roshwald 2006) and, more generally, to the role of the Biblical texts in fostering secular political power and its desacralisation. In this case, too, it is, however, a matter of limited, simplistic, frequently anachronistic perspectives which must be reconsidered in all their complexity. This is not the place for detailed analysis of this issue but it may be worth mentioning the words of American scholar and Rabbi Danya Ruttenberg, according to whom '"Judeo-Christian" isn't a thing. It a) positions Jews & Christians against Muslims, is Islamophobic b) elides Christian oppression & murder of Jews over more than 1000 years & c) ignores Jewish civilization worldwide & facts of key Jewish developments in Middle East & N[orth] Africa',[19] as well as in North America and other contexts.

19 Tweet by Danya Ruttenberg, 27 January 2019, https://twitter.com/theradr/status/1089589999920660484. For a more thoroughgoing analysis, see Neusner and Sonn 1999.

The earliest communications between Europeans and native American peoples were, for that matter, in 'the language of Islam': when Christopher Columbus's (1451–1506) interpreter, Luís de Torres (?–1493), a Spanish Jew, approached the indigenous peoples of Taínos ('friendly people'), he did so in Arabic.[20]

In addition to being misleading, the widespread tendency to refer to a 'Western Jewish-Christian tradition' risks accentuating dangerous antagonisms and 'watershed' phenomena at the expense of a greater understanding of the shared historical legacy underlying the three largest mono-theistic religions.

A powerful confirm of this can be seen in Epic of Gilgamesh (c. 2100), a Mesopotamian poem containing many of the themes – including the myth of the 'universal flood', Noah's Ark, the Garden of Eden – later included virtually in their entirety in the Bible and other religious texts. A further significant example can be found in the 'holy city' *par excellence:* Jerusalem. As noted in a study published by the University of Bar-Ilan, 'Canaanite Jerusalem had two holy sites; both were above and outside the city walls. Shalem was probably worshipped in the area of the Temple Mount, which later became the holiest site for the Jews and the third most holy site for Moslems' (Shalem 1997). The idea of the rosary itself was taken from Muslims in Spain who were inspired by the prayerbeads of Buddhists in Central Asia, who in turn borrowed the idea from Brahmans in Hindu India (cfr. Juergensmeyer 2006: 4). Religions, like a number of issues relating to 'cultural heritage' and other aspects mentioned in this work, are thus themselves the result of human accumulation: a process which, particularly in our times, is not always understood in all its complexity and potential.

References

Amato, Giuliano and Carlo Cardia (2015), 'Carta dei valori della cittadinanza e dell'integrazione', in Carlo Cardia Giuseppe Dalla Torre, eds, *Comunità islamiche in Italia. Identità e forme giuridiche*, Torino, Giappichelli, p. 597–615

Blaut, James Morris (1993), *The Colonizer's Model of the World*, New York/ London, The Guilford Press

20 When Columbus landed on 12 October 1492 on one of the islands of the modern Bahamas he believed he had reached the Indies and persisted in this belief until his death. The continent had been inhabited by indigenous peoples for thousands of years – who clearly did not understand Arabic – and was 'discovered' many centuries before Columbus by Vikings, Scandinavians and other peoples.

Blaut, James Morris (2000), *Eight Eurocentric Historians*, New York/London, The Guilford Press

Bondi, Sandro Filippo (2001), 'Political and Administrative Organization', in Sabatino Moscati, ed., *The Phoenicians*, London, I.B. Tauris, p. 153–159

Burke, Peter (1998), *The European Renaissance. Centres and Peripheries*, Oxford, Blackwell

Cardini, Franco (2001), *Europa e Islam. Storia di un malinteso*, 4th ed., Roma/ Bari, Laterza

Dejung, Christof, David Motadel and Jürgen Osterhammel (2019), 'Worlds of the Bourgeoisie', in David Motadel, Christof Dejung JürgenOsterhammel, eds, *The Global Bourgeoisie. The Rise of the Middle Classes in the Age of Empire*, Princeton, Princeton University Press, 2019, p. 1–39

Detti, Tommaso (2019), 'L'egemonia mondiale dell'Europa', in *Il mestiere di storico*, Vol. 11, No. 1, p. 71–72

Euben, Roxanne L. (2006), *Journeys to the Other Shore. Muslim and Western Travelers in Search of Knowledge*, Princeton, Princeton University Press

Frank, Andre Gunder (1998), *ReOrient. Global Economy in the Asian Age*, Berkeley, University of California Press

Gentile, Emilio (2018), *Ascesa e declino dell'Europa nel mondo: 1898–1918*, Milano, Garzanti

Gramsci, Antonio (1971), *Selections from the Prison Notebooks*, edited by Quintin Hoare and Geoffrey Nowell Smith, New York, International Publishers

Goody, Jack (1996), *The East in the West*, Cambridge, Cambridge University Press

Goody, Jack (2006), *The Theft of History*, Cambridge, Cambridge University Press

Hegel, Georg Wilhelm Friedrich (1956 [1837]), *The Philosophy of History*, Mineola, Dover Publications

Henze, Paul B. (2000), *Layers of Time. A History of Ethiopia*, London, Hurst

Hermes, Nizar F. (2012), *The (European) Other in Medieval Arabic Literature and Culture. Ninth-twelfth Century AD*, New York, Palgrave Macmillan

Hobson, John M. (2006), 'Revealing the Cosmopolitan Side of Oriental Europe. The Eastern Origins of European Civilisation', in Gerard Delanty, ed., *Europe and Asia Beyond East and West*, London/New York, Routledge, p. 107–119

Hornblower, Simon (1992), 'Creation and Development of Democratic Institutions in Ancient Greece', in John Dunn, ed., *Democracy. The*

Unfinished Journey, 508 BC to AD 1993, Oxford, Oxford University Press, p. 1–16

Huizinga, Johan (1936), 'A Definition of the Concept of History', in Raymond Klibansky and H.J. Paton, eds, *Philosophy and History. Essays presented to Ernst Cassirer*, Oxford, Clarendon Press, p. 1–10

James, Cyril L.R. (1989), *The Black Jacobins. Toussaint L'Ouverture and the San Domingo Revolution*, 2nd ed. revised, New York, Vintage Books

Jones, Eric L. (1981), *The European Miracle. Environments, Economies, and Geopolitics in the History of Europe and Asia*, Cambridge, Cambridge University Press

Juergensmeyer, Mark (2006), 'Thinking Globally About Religion', in Mark Juergensmeyer, ed., *The Oxford Handbook of Global Religions*, Oxford, Oxford University Press, p. 3–12

König, Daniel G. (2015), *Arabic-Islamic Views of the Latin West. Tracing the Emergence of Medieval Europe*, Oxford, Oxford University Press

Lamprakos, Michele (2015), *Building a World Heritage City. Sanaa, Yemen*, Farnham/Burlington, Ashgate

Lewis, Bernard (1982), *The Muslim Discovery of Europe*, New York/ London, Norton

Lewis, Bernard (1993), *Islam and the West*, Oxford, Oxford University Press

Lowe, Robert (1878), 'Imperialism', in *The Fortnightly Review*, Vol. 24, new series, p. 453–465, https://hdl.handle.net/2027/osu.32435054416698

Matar, Nabil, ed. (2003), *In the Lands of the Christians. Arabic Travel Writing in the Seventeenth Century*, New York/London, Routledge

Meiksins Wood, Ellen (2011), *Citizens to Lords. A Social History of Western Political Thought from Antiquity to the Late Middle Ages*, London/ New York, Verso

Mishra, Pankaj (2012), *From the Ruins of Empire. The Intellectuals Who Remade Asia*, New York, Farrar, Straus & Giroux

Munro-Hay, Stuart C. (1991), *Aksum: An African Civilisation of Late Antiquity*, Edinburgh, Edinburgh University Press

Neusner, Jacob and Tamara Sonn (1999), *Comparing Religions through Law: Judaism and Islam*, London/New York, Routledge

Park, Peter K.J. (2013), *Africa, Asia, and the History of Philosophy. Racism in the Formation of the Philosophical Canon, 1780–1830*, Albany, State University of New York Press

Paul, Gregor (1993), 'Equivalent Axioms of Aristotelian, or Traditional European, and Later Mohist Logic: An Argument in Favor of the

Universality of Logic and Rationality', in Hans Lenk and GregorPaul, eds, *Epistemological Issues in Classical Chinese Philosophy*, Albany, State University of New York Press, p. 119–135

Phillipson, David W. (2012), *Foundations of an African Civilization. Aksum and the Northern Horn, 1000 BC – AD 1300*, Woodbridge, James Currey

Polybius (1923), *The Histories. Vol. III: Books 5–8*, translated by W.R. Paton, London, Heinemann / New York, Putnam's sons

Porceddu, Sebastian et al. (2018), 'Algol as Horus in the Cairo Calendar: The Possible Means and the Motives of the Observations', in *Open Astronomy*, Vol. 27, No. 1, pp. 232–263, https://doi.org/10.1515/astro-2018-0033

Roshwald, Mordecai (2006), 'The Biblical Roots of Democracy', in *Diogenes*, Vol. 53, No. 4, p. 139–151

Sen, Amartya (2003), 'Democracy and Its Global Roots', in *The New Republic*, 6 October 2003, p. 28

Shalem, Yisrael (1997), *Jerusalem: Life Throughout the Ages in a Holy City. History of Jerusalem from Its Beginning to David*, Bar-Ilan University, Ingeborg Rennert Center for Jerusalem Studies, https://www.biu.ac.il/JS/rennert/history_2.html

Smallacombe, Sonia (2000), 'On Display for its Aesthetic Beauty: How Western Institutions Fabricate Knowledge about Aboriginal Cultural Heritage', in Duncan Ivison, Paul Patton and Will Sanders, eds, *Political Theory and the Rights of Indigenous Peoples*, Cambridge, Cambridge University Press, p. 152–162

Stockwell, Stephen (2010), 'Before Athens: Early Popular Government in Phoenician and Greek City States', in *Geopolitics, History, and International Relations*, Vol. 2, No. 2, 2010, p. 123–135

Subrahmanyam, Sanjay (2015), 'On Early Modern Historiography', in Jerry H. Bentley, Sanjay Subrahmanyam, Merry E. Wiesner-Hanks, eds, The Cambridge World History. Vol. 6: *The Construction of a Global World, 1400–1800 CE. Part 2: Patterns of Change*, Cambridge, Cambridge University Press, p. 425–445

Subrahmanyam, Sanjay (2019), *Empires Between Islam and Christianity, 1500–1800*, Albany, State University of New York Press

Tagliaferri, Teodoro (2019), 'L'espansione europea nella prospettiva della nuova storia globale', in *Il mestiere di storico*, Vol. 11, No. 1, p. 5–25

Trevor-Roper, Hugh R. (1965), *The Rise of Christian Europe*, London, Thames and Hudson

Vicente Rabanaque, Teresa (2015), 'From Artistic Expression As Individual Capability to Cultural Heritage: A Collective Legacy's Rights and

Responsibilities', in Koji Nakatogawa et al., eds, *Discussing Capabilities, Emotions and Values. A Cross-cultural Perspective*, Sapporo, Hokkaido University, p. 89–102

Wallerstein, Immanuel (1997), 'Eurocentrism and its Avatars: The Dilemmas of Social Science', in *Sociological Bulletin*, Vol. 46, No. 1, March, p. 21–39

Contributors

Francesco Bandarin is an Architect and Urban Planner. He has been Director of the UNESCO World Heritage Centre (2000–2010) and UNESCO Assistant Director-General for Culture (2010–2018). He is currently Special Advisor of Special Advisor of the Director-General of the International Centre for the Study of the Preservation and Restoration of Cultural Property (ICCROM) and Senior Advisor of the Aga Khan Trust for Culture (AKTC).

Stefano de Martino is Professor of Hittitology at the University of Turin; he is Director of Centro Ricerche Archeologiche e Scavi di Torino per il Medio Oriente e l'Asia and has collaborated to the renovation of the Iraq Museum in Baghdad.

Ettore Greco is Executive Vice President of the IAI and also Head of the Multilateralism and Global Governance Programme of the institute. He was Director of the IAI from 2008 to 2017.

Lorenzo Kamel is Associate Professor of History at the University of Turin and director of IAI's *Research Studies*. He taught in several universities in Europe, the US, and the Middle East, and was a Postdoc Fellow at Harvard University for two years, and a Marie Curie Experienced Researcher at the Albert-Ludwigs-Universität Freiburg.

Elijah J. Magnier is a veteran war-zone correspondent and political analyst with over 38 years' experience in the Middle East and North Africa. Extended fieldwork in Lebanon, Bosnia, Iraq, Iran, Sudan, Libya and Syria, created his extensive network of trusted military and political contacts. Magnier specializes in real-time reporting and in-depth analysis of political, strategic and military planning, terrorism and counter-terrorism.

Omar Mohammed is a historian from Mosul known to the world as the founder of the Mosul Eye platform that documented ISIS' occupation of Mosul. He received his M.A in Middle East History from Mosul University and is finishing his Ph.D. in the Ottoman History of Mosul at the École des Hautes Études en Sciences Sociales in Paris. He is also a lecturer at SciencesPo University in Cultural Heritage Diplomacy. He is also a senior consultant to UNESCO.

Nicolò Russo Perez is the coordinator of the International Affairs Programme at the Compagnia di San Paolo Foundation. Previously he worked at the European Commission, at the International Labour Organization and was a senior associate fellow at the EUISS in Paris.

Abdul Salam Taha is an Iraqi researcher and writer in the field of archeology; he is an architect and an expert in ancient Iraqi architecture, and historical building maintenance and preservation.

Abbreviations

AKDN	Aga Khan Development Network
AKTC	Aga Khan Trust for Culture
AQI	Al-Qaeda in Iraq
ARC-WH	Arab Regional Centre for World Heritage
BDTNS	Base de datos de textos neo-Sumerios (Database of Neo-Sumerian Texts)
BRILA	Bureau for the Recovery of the Iraqi Looted Antiquities
CIA	Central Intelligence Agency
CRAST	Centro Ricerche Archeologiche e Scavi di Torino per il Medio Oriente e l'Asia
DAI	Deutsches Archäologisches Institut
DGAM	Directorate-General of Antiquities and Museums
DOC	Directorate of the Old City
EDUU	Education and Cultural Heritage Enhancement for Social Cohesion in Iraq
GHF	Global Heritage Fund
GIZ	Deutsche Gesellschaft für Internationale Zusammenarbeit
GTZ	Deutsche Gesellschaft für Technische Zusammenarbeit
ICCROM	International Centre for the Study of the Preservation and Restoration of Cultural Property
ICOMOS	International Council on Monuments and Sites
IRGC	Iranian Revolutionary Guard Corps
IS	Islamic State
ISI	Islamic State of Iraq
ISIL	Islamic State of Iraq and the Levant
ISIS	Islamic State of Iraq and Sham
ISIS	Islamic State of Iraq and Syria
MAECI	Ministero degli Affari esteri e della Cooperazione internazionale
MIBACT	Ministero per i Beni e le attività culturali e per il Turismo
NGO	Non-governmental organization
NRK	Norwegian Broadcasting Corporation
PKK	Kurdistan Workers' Party
PMF	Popular Mobilization Force
SBAH	State Board of Antiquities and Heritage

U4H	Unity for Heritage
UCL	University College London
UK	United Kingdom
UN	United Nations
UNDP	United Nations Development Programme
UNESCO	United Nations Educational, Scientific and Cultural Organization
UNIDROIT	International Institute for the Unification of Private Law
UNITAR	United Nations Institute for Training and Research
US	United States
WHC	World Heritage Centre
WMF	World Monuments Fund
YPG	Kurdish People's Protection Units

GLOBAL POLITICS AND SECURITY

Series Editor:
Prof. Lorenzo Kamel,
University of Turin's History Department,
and Istituto Affari Internazionali (IAI)

"Global Politics and Security" publishes high-quality books authored by leading academics, think-tankers and policymakers on topical questions in international relations and contemporary history, ranging from diplomacy and security, to development, economy, migration, energy and climate. The series publishes works produced by the Istituto Affari Internazionali (IAI), Italy's leading foreign policy think-tank, as well as by authors affiliated to other international think tanks or universities. The aim is to promote deeper knowledge of emerging issues and trends through constant exchange between the worlds of academia and practice. Publications include original monographs and edited volumes which combine a grasp of the past, an understanding of present dynamics, and a vision about potential futures.

Vol. 1 Lorenzo Colantoni, Giuseppe Montesano, Nicolò Sartori (eds): Empowering Africa. Access to power in the African continent

Vol. 2 Aybars Görgülü, Gulsah Dark Kahyaoğlu (eds): The Remaking of the Euro-Mediterranean Vision. Challenging Eurocentrism with Local Perceptions in the Middle East and North Africa.

Vol. 3 Leila Simona Talani, Matilde Rosina (eds): Tidal Waves? The Political Economy of Populism and Migration in Europe.

Vol. 4 Nicola Bilotta, Simone Romano (eds): The Rise of Tech Giants. A Game Changer in Global Finance and Politics.

Vol. 5 Lorenzo Kamel (ed.): The Middle East: Thinking About and Beyond Security and Stability.

Vol. 6 Lorenzo Kamel (ed.): Collapse and Rebirth of Cultural Heritage: The Case of Syria and Iraq.

www.peterlang.com